INTEGRATIVE

ARCHAEOLOGY

INTEGRATIVE ARCHAEOLOGY

The Essential Guide For Visiting
Sacred Sites and Power Places

Luminous Antonio

PORTALS of TRANSCENDENCE
P U B L I S H I N G

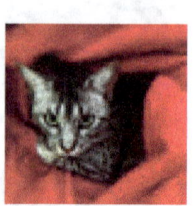

PORTALS of TRANSCENDENCE
P U B L I S H I N G

www.LuminousAntonio.com

Copyright © 2013, All rights reserved.

ISBN: 979-8-9871-8000-6 (Print)

ISBN: 979-8-9871800-1-3 (eBook)

Third Edition © 2022

Library of Congress Control Number: 2012914989

Cover design: Luminous Antonio

Images and artwork by Luminous Antonio, all rights reserved. Images noted with and * after the title were taken from open sources or purchased from iStock Photo.

Third Edition Printed on acid-free paper.

I dedicate this book to my amazing and beautiful parents and everyone else who has inspired me, by whatever means, to look more deeply into my Self.

Luminous Antonio

Cast a stone in the oceans of the past
when time was new
and today was yet to be lived

Earth is where the ancestors planted dreams
at the core of pyramids
in monuments and myths

Ancient glyphs chiseled loose from stone walls
laid down for memory's sake
reminders of truths in moments of potential madness

Long ago the ancient ones scripted a garden of paradise
called planet earth

Avatars and ancient gods bartered for time
while spilling dreams like gentle rain
welcoming the spring
the flowering

Breath of Life activates the sound
stirs stories written upon our bones
stories of this time
that have come to us only in dream time
until now

Telepathic language travels from thought form
into manifestation
faster than the speed of light

Homecoming
we are from a world indivisible
a mirror of wholeness
BREATHE

Luminous Antonio, 1994

ACKNOWLEDGMENTS

EASTER ISLAND, RAPA NUI ISLAND, CHILE

Committing this material to the page has always been going on inside me. I have forgotten more than I will ever remember, and the journey of a writer is life-long including so many seminars, teachers, books, and experiences that paved the way to materialize this work.

I extend deep and heartfelt thanks and gratitude to everyone who has touched my life. Every relationship and experience helped me reach a higher perspective and dive deeper within myself—here are a few: In 1982, Deanna Pedroli told me I should really write down what I was saying—and so I began carrying a notebook. The San Francisco Art Institute and Multidimensional Research and Expansion gave me languages for my experience—visual, emotional, psychic, and verbal. Jesus Christ and other avatars, scores of beings, and ancestors, invisible and ever present continue to make the impossible easy.

Nancy Beckett (Lakeside Writing Studio, Chicago) was foundational in all aspects of writing and assembling a book. Jacalyn S. Burke enthusiastically inspired the rewrite of this book.

J.J. Hurtak, and Desiree Hurtak, for their presence and insights.

I thank the Sacred Sites and Power Places and the beings that inhabit them who consistently inspire and inform me. Although I have painted, documented, visited, and created performance art about Sacred Places for decades, I had no idea I would write this book.

TO THE READER

Explorers, travelers, spiritual explorers, and those interested in archaeology, hidden histories, ancestral connections, sacred sites, power places, holy places, mythology, practical shamanism, personal, spiritual, and psychic development, ancient cultures and alternative historical narratives.

I am not alone in this quest. So strong is the pull that people spend their lives and resources to get a glimpse, a remembrance about who and what came before. Sifting through clues using scientific and intuitive means, sorting through myths, delving into the technology necessary to move and carve monolithic stones, determine precise placement and age of sites. It may be that in this way, we can further define ourselves, ultimately reclaim our divinity. It is as if something has been lost and needs to be found and its importance is vital to the continuation of life itself.

Sometime in 2008 or so I was sitting in the lounge at the hotel attached to the airport in Lima, enduring the inevitable long wait for that night flight to LAX. I decided to write a "pamphlet" on travel to sacred sites and power places. I visualized this as a thin book, saddle stapled, easy.

By the time I got home I realized I have been an explorer and documenter of the places of the past—and I had plenty of research available! This was something I always did, did it naturally and consistently throughout my life. Beginning in the 1980's, I would sometimes include others on my adventures and surreptitiously became a facilitator of sacred travel. My travel has always been inspired by archaeological sites, sacred sites and power places.

Realizing my material would need much more than a pamphlet presentation, over the next couple years I wrote a 200-page book on Sacred Sites and Power Places. The very last chapter was called Integrative Archaeology – understanding, visiting, and connecting with the healing, wisdom, and power of these sites. It felt like that was what people needed to hear about most. I clipped off the last chapter and published my first edition of this book in 2012.

Has our consciousness degenerated over time leaving us with a broken operating system or are we the best we have ever been? Was there a breakdown of memory? What were we about in the distant past, what did we dream and intend? What did we know that we have forgotten? And why is it so important to so many of us that we continue a quest for what lies beneath?

Each one of us sees, feels, intuits, and understands the world around us a bit differently. The same is true when exploring our distant pasts and ancestral homes. Whatever you divine is valid and will doubtless be useful to you – and maybe others. What lies beneath the amorphous layers of time draws our curiosity and will help define our future.

Diverse and constant new research continues to lift the veil over our past. Still, we sort among remaining fragments and we are left with more questions than answers. If you are drawn to explore, study, visit, remote view or connect with ancient and prehistoric sites and civilizations, this book is for you. I hope to inspire you to become part of the great adventure.

IMAGE OF HORUS, TEMPLE OF EDFU, EGYPT

INTEGRATIVE ARCHAEOLOGY

Integrative Archaeology empowers us to reclaim our innate abilities to connect with the Earth, Sacred Sites and Power Places; ultimately ourselves. It is a personal, multidimensional, multi-sensory search and exploration into the invisible realms of existence to discover our true origins, with all that entails; the recovery of hidden histories, lost customs, forgotten abilities and practices When these gifts are returned to us, we access deeper meanings beyond the material evidence of ancient and prehistoric civilizations and cultures.

Integrative Archaeology delivers what explorers of Sacred Places are seeking – something that traditional tourism cannot provide - access to the invisible realms of existence, hidden spiritual wealth, life-changing personal messages and the unique stories Sacred Places have to reveal.

It offers deep insights about Sacred Places and how to connect to them. It opens access to the healing, wisdom and transformational powers of Sacred Places. Integrative Archaeology also shares preparations, diving skills and exercises to increase intuitive abilities, and unveils practical shamanism as a way to access the spiritual wealth of Sacred Places. It is a modality that supports an inward focus, confidence, and trust.

Traditional Archaeology continues to give us a broad-stroke view of the past, and the events that conditioned us. How we harnessed the environment brought about the domestication of plants, animals, and developed agricultural systems. Traditional Archaeology helps us to understand the processes of becoming urbanized and how we developed complex societies. It serves to understand our basic needs.

But it cannot answer questions like: Were there greater civilizations before ours? Why do indigenous peoples speak about Sky Gods? Why were the ancients drawing what appeared to be spacemen on cave walls? What were individuals/societies questing to connect with or understand? Traditional Archaeology's theories also could not explain why certain artifacts and structures that fall outside of normal timelines and categories existed.

In recent decades there has been an explosion of new explorers who are compelled to find those answers. This movement would come to be known as Alternative Archaeology. Researchers from all walks and professions utilized new and improved scientific methods for locating and dating sites and items. Studies in human DNA coupled with breakthroughs in understanding our holographic universe have added to the mix. Amongst this group there has been a lot of talk and theories proposed, and some science to back this up. And yet, something is lacking.

Integrative Archaeology bridges the gap between Traditional Archaeology and Alternative Archaeology. It offers a spiritual path because humanity's journey from its unknowable distant beginning has been a spiritual one. It seeks to empower the individual to tap into their innate abilities and have the courage to find answers about the past.

Alternative Archaeology and Integrative Archaeology hold a powerful idea in common. Namely, that greater civilizations existed in the past. Another idea they share is that human beings have been around far longer than is traditionally asserted. Yet another idea is that we didn't come about through a slow, blind process of evolution.

These ideas are gaining ground both in terms of evidence and popularity. The History channel, Netflix, Amazon, and You Tube all regularly stream shows about ancient civilizations, alien gods and cover-ups in terms of human origin. The reason is simple - people are consuming that type of content in greater numbers because somewhere deep inside of them they know that we have not been told or shown the absolute truth about our species.

Ancient sites hold many mysteries. Can we ever truly know the intimate history of a place without living concurrently in it, without connecting spiritually with it? Do Sacred Places contain, like holographic records, a map of our past? Can our DNA – when it has been enhanced to a higher frequency by sacred knowledge and shamanic practice – act as a divine key?

Integrative Archaeologists will tell you – yes. The answer is hidden in plain sight, right under our noses.

AUTHOR'S STATEMENT

Prose, poetry, paintings, photographs, and insights are all mediums I have used in this book to attempt to shed light on the varied and auspicious times of our true origins. Many indigenous people, and others, believe firmly that we came from the stars. Other stories tell of emerging from the earth or the center of the earth. Creation stories and myths speak of our genesis, challenges, abilities, and destinies.

As more remains and sites are discovered, our origins seem to slide further into a distant past. Why look back to times long forgotten?

It is my belief that our ancestors live on through us, connecting us to a vast network of knowledge, wisdom, and wellbeing. Their lives, like ours, have not been lived in vain to be forgotten and turned to dust.

Our future selves embody the enlightened remembrance of who we are and what we are capable of. We are divine, godlike beings, with powers and abilities of magical proportions. We are destined to live heaven on earth.

These topics are so much bigger than any form of expression can illuminate. Hopefully, this material will inspire and awaken in you a quest, personal and planetary, to lift out of the trappings of consensus reality and realize an expanded sense of self.

Contents

1
MYTH, MYSTERY AND MAGIC IN THE PAST

SPHINX BEFORE DAWN, EGYPT

MYTH, MYSTERY AND MAGIC IN THE PAST

SPHINX AT DAYBREAK, EGYPT

It is by dim candlelight we wind our way through prehistory seeking clues and remembrances of how it all began. Ancestors stand behind us in a longer line than any genealogy chart will ever reveal. Darkened hallways, tombs, pyramids, and the earth itself hold the secrets and clues left for us to unravel and help us understand who our real ancestors were.

We are captivated by our ancestry, our lineage—especially what exists before recorded history. There are no definitive answers to the question of who came before, who originally built what remains of the structures of the past. Your research will find unique answers and insights, and every bit of it is valid. There are so many books to read by researchers and explorers of sacred sites and power places. I encourage you to read and study the information out there. I hope to inspire you to initiate your own search and treasure the answers you find.

Drawing up a chronology of this obscure past we rely upon the myths and stories and works handed down through the ages. There are always discrepancies and the numbers and times will rarely match up. Yet, there is enough to give us a glimpse and stir the imagination and memory.

Traditional archaeology points to Sumeria as the beginning of civilization. However, I believe we are much older as a species and have been here longer. Consider this timeline an extremely broad brushstroke of our possible past:

Lemurians . . . . 34.25 million years ago
Atlanteans . . . . .4,500,000 years ago
Denisovans . . . . 200,000 to 50,000 years ago
Last Ice Age . . . . 12,000 Years ago
Deluge . . . . 5,000 to 7,000 years ago
Sumerians . . . . 7,000 – 4,000 years ago

Are we descended from gods? "God" specifically refers to the Abrahamic God/Yahweh/Allah followed by the three major monotheistic faiths: Judaism, Christianity, and Islam. In Christianity there is also God the Father, The Son (Jesus) and the Holy Spirit, making the trinity. In monotheistic thought, God is conceived of as the supreme being, creator deity, and principal object of faith; omniscient (all-knowing), omnipotent (all-powerful), omnipresent (all-present) and as having an eternal and necessary existence.

There are many references in the bible to man being created in the image and likeness of God. The King James Version of the bible (*Wisdom of Solomon* 2:23) states:

For God created man to be immortal and made him to be an image of his own eternity.

Polytheistic religious systems such as Hinduism follow many gods. The legion of gods spanning polytheistic religions, myths and stories of the past are also credited with immortality, seemingly magical abilities, and superpowers. Beings in the past who come to us through legend, myth, and iconography, in my opinion, did exist. Whether from the stars, other planets, distant pasts, or parallel universes, they made their mark and left reminders and traces of what is possible.

As an example, the powers of the Greek Gods are outlined as:

- Immortality – they did not die
- Transformation or shape shifting
- Enhanced intelligence
- The ability and power to move from one place to another in an instant (one equivalent would be Teleportation)
- Powers to manipulate animals to obey their commands
- Powers to manipulate the weather
- Powers to become invisible
- Powers to create fantastic beings and weapons with supernatural powers
- Their blood was a bright unearthly fluid called Ichor that had the power of producing new life

Undeniably, God, goddesses and gods, divine and semi-divine beings were elevated and expressed differently than we do today. We were made in the image and likeness of God. What happened? Have we forgotten our legacy? Have we been systematically conditioned to be less than we are intended to be?

I believe we are descended from God(s), and it is our task to remember who we are and what we are capable of – and to integrate that back into our lives today.

It is a common belief of indigenous and other cultures throughout the world that life/civilization was created by extra-celestials, gods, who came from the sky or stars or even beneath the earth. Ancient Egyptians also believed their civilization was born with the Sky Gods who existed thousands of years before the human pharaonic dynasties.

Berossus, a 3rd century BC Chaldean priest wrote three books in Greek about the creation and the early history of the world. Fragments of the Turin papyrus, lists of kings written on the walls of Saqqara, Abydos, and Karnak, leave indelible clues from the

KING'S LIST ABYDOS, EGYPT

past. Both Manetho and Berossus wrote of the progression of rulers of Egypt from the Gods to the first human pharaoh.

Other pre-dynastic genealogies include Eusebius, bishop of Caesarea in Palestine, Byzantine chronicler Syncellus and Africanus.

TURIN KING LIST

The Turin King List (or Turin Royal Canon), an ancient papyrus, states ten Neteru, or gods, reigned for hundreds of years each, for a total of 23,200 years. After this comes a list dedicated to Shemsu Hor, the Followers of Horus, who reigned a total of 13,400 years. The first human pharaoh of Egypt was Narmar (also known as Menes) who began his rule in 3150 BCE.

Other King's Lists appear on the walls of Karnac, Saqqara and Abydos. While there is some controversy about what appears to be excessively long reigns of the divine and semi-divine rulers we can look to the bible where prophets such as Enoch live over 360 years. Science offers us some possibilities for what must have been a much slower aging process. Lower density, different terrestrial gravity, DNA that was different or better protected, other ways of measuring time, a lack of disease.

SHEMSU HOR

Before the Sky Gods left and returned to the stars, they co-existed with a group of mysterious rulers known as the Shemsu Hor (Perhaps the legendary Atlanteans?). Known as the Followers of Horus, the Shemsu Hor were semi-divine kings, priests, and keepers of sacred knowledge. They are sometimes referred to as members of the first ancient secret society. They were present in Egypt during the Golden Ages of the original divine kings, and they remained there long after these kings ascended back to the stars.

HORUS GIVING LIFE TO THE PHARAOH, EGYPT

Companions of Horus, the Shemsu Hor (from 4000BC) were described as wearing the masks of falcons or wolves. Imagery suggests they may have been the initiators of the sophisticated and remarkable Pharaonic dynasties that sprang into being without a recorded developmental past.

Found at the temple of Edfu in Egypt, the so-called Building Texts say the Shemsu Hor were a race of highly endowed sages living on ten prediluvian islands (Atlantis?). Thoth, known to the Greeks as Hermes and the Romans as Mercury, was one of their elders.

The Shemsu Hor inherited sacred knowledge of the pyramids, the Sphinx, and the surrounding energy fields. Who were these secretive rulers of divine origin who gave people the knowledge of astronomy, mathematics, agriculture, and architecture? In my opinion, they were the Atlanteans.

MANETHO (THOTH, TEHUTI, HERMES)

From Michael Doreal's translation of the Emerald Tablets:

> *I, Thoth, the Atlantean, master of mysteries, keeper of records, mighty king, magician, living from generation to generation, being able to pass through the halls of Amenti, set down for the guidance for those that are to come after, these records of the mighty wisdom of Atlantis …*

THOTH*

Egyptian High Priest Manetho (Ma-N-Thoth), 3rd century BCE, had access to the library at Alexandria and was considered the Master of Secrets. He wrote a 30-volume history of Egypt in Greek for the Pharaoh known as the "Aegiptiaca" which cited the pre-dynasties as being of divine origin.

20,000 works are attributed to Manetho, the master scribe and historian who claimed the divine gods ruled from 33,894 to 23,642 BC.

Manetho's details on the "divine" dynasties are divided into three categories: Gods, Heroes, and "Manes".

GODS - divided into seven sections each having a god at its head, including Horus, Anubis, Thoth, Ptah, Osiris and Ra and that "these gods who originated from Earth then became celestial and associated with the stars as they reached heaven". The reference "originating from Earth" recalls the possibility of a subterranean realm of the planet. Osiris himself says in The Book of Coming Out by Day "The tunnels of the earth gave me birth"

HEROS - beings with supernatural terrestrial powers. Shemsu Hor.

"MANES" (also called "Khus"} and "Spirits of the Dead" were glorious beings corresponding to the spirits of ancestors revered in other cultures.

Manetho is considered the father of Egyptology and his dating of the dynasties is considered perfectly reliable as it relates to the "official" viewpoint of recognized historical dynasties. However, any reference to the pre-existing divine dynasties is carefully avoided and generally denied by traditional Egyptology

WHAT DOES IT MEAN TO US?

I provide these examples to inspire you to look beyond, beneath, above, and below for your answers to our past. What would these beings – Thoth, the Sky Gods, the demi-gods, the Shemsu Hor – tell us if we could talk to them right now – today? What questions would we ask? What do we want to see, know, or understand about the reign of the gods, their wisdom, intentions, and abilities? Healing? Longevity? Super-consciousness? Whatever we would like to tap into or integrate is available. What knowledge or magic can we incorporate into our lives today?

INTEGRATIVE ARCHAEOLOGY PROVIDES A WINDOW TO THE PAST

Integrative Archaeology empowers us to reclaim our innate abilities to connect with the Earth, Sacred Sites and Power Places; ultimately ourselves. It is a personal, multidimensional, multi-sensory search and exploration into the invisible realms of existence to discover our true origins, with all that entails; the recovery of hidden histories, lost customs, forgotten abilities and practices. When these gifts are returned to us, we access deeper meanings beyond the material evidence of ancient and prehistoric civilizations and cultures.

TERMS OF ENGAGEMENT

Tourists don't know where they've been; travelers don't know where they're going. Paul Theroux

Tourism is the economic backbone of many countries and cities around the world. In most instances, tour providers—both traditional and spiritual—are focused on the skillful management of people in and out of a variety of conveyances and locations according to a timetable to fulfill a schedule. The nature of tourism is to have the visitor see as much as possible of a country or place during their visit. During this sightseeing, photos are taken, many words are spoken, and the tourist can say, "Yes, I have been there."

A traveler will take care in planning their journey and remains open to the adventure, the unknown. What about the spiritual explorer who makes a journey based upon a calling and desires a deep connection with sacred places?

> *The spiritual explorer is seeking something tourism does not address—that which is hidden and invisible.*

It takes an easy, relaxed, multi-sensory interaction with sacred places to access what lies in invisible realms. Often, long distances are traveled at great expense and the last thing we want to experience is being flashed through a site at lightning speed with a guide parroting stories and pointing out what they feel is important for us to see.

> *Integrative Archaeologists mine the spiritual wealth of sacred places.*

During my lifetime of travel to sacred places around the world I have personally witnessed increasing closures and restrictions for visitors due to the sheer numbers of people traveling and visiting these sites. Unfortunately, many are uninformed and unaware of how to treat the earth and the sites themselves.

ULURU | AYERS ROCK | AUSTRALIA*

Erosion due to dismantling, graffiti and trash are just a few of the assaults on these heritage sites. ATVs and other off-road vehicles destroy roads and vegetation. Visitors enthusiastically climb pyramids and rocks not realizing the erosion created by millions of footsteps.

Many visitors are not even aware of the sacredness of the sites they visit, the indigenous people who revere and utilize the sites for ceremony and prayer or the delicacy of the land and structures themselves. Their quest may be simply to have a photo of themselves at the site and be able to say they have been there.

The Anangu Aboriginal people placed signs at the base of Australia's Uluru, formerly Ayers Rock, strongly discouraging climbing their sacred cultural site. Many tourists do it anyway, eating, drinking and relieving themselves on the way. To preserve areas of historical and spiritual importance, aboriginal people are crying for restrictions against public access to heritage sites.

ULURU | OIL ON CANVAS | Painting by Luminous Antonio

Worldwide, we have seen cultural and sacred heritage sites destroyed by natural disasters and war. Yet, our greatest threat is tourism spawning an ongoing daily assault that initiates restrictions, closures, and outright loss of the sites themselves.

Machu Picchu, which seems to be on everyone's "bucket list" cannot withstand the impact of hundreds of thousands of visitors a year. Physical burdens on the site are requiring extra infrastructure to support the newcomers and limitations on entry.

Angkor Wat at the BaYon Temple features approximately 50 intricately carved stone towers revealing the four faces of the Bodhisattva Avalokiteshvara on most of them.

I spent a couple hours at this site and hundreds of people were busy vying for photo ops, waiting for their turn at a certain structure or window. I did not observe even one person looking at the site or connecting with it in any way, other than as a backdrop for their selfies or photos. This is the prevailing consciousness of the tourist. Meanwhile, to acquire these photos, they are climbing around, sitting on

BAYON TEMPLE, ANGKOR WAT, CAMBODIA

walls, even making videos of themselves doing acrobatics. The same was true at Angkor Wat and every other temple visited in Cambodia – photographs were the priority and tourists felt it was OK to block the entry for others so they could get a good shot.

What are we to do? As conscious, sensitive, and aware explorers, we can demonstrate the behaviors that protect these cultural heritage sites and share information with others when it is appropriate to do so.

I live in a tourist town, and the destruction, trash and rampant disregard for the land, sites and residents is appalling. Local government does little or nothing to discourage the outright destruction of our pristine land and places, for fear, I suppose, of driving off the tourists. Those of us that live here are left to endure the onslaught and clean up the mountains of trash left behind. The U.S. Forest Service removes tons (real tons, not an exaggeration) of dirty diapers from the canyon each year. Wouldn't a $1000 fine for littering clean this up fast?

Read Chapter 10 of this book – Outdoor and Site Etiquette; take it to heart and share it liberally in whatever way possible.

2

SACRED SITES AND POWER PLACES

STONEHENGE, ENGLAND

Specific planetary locations have been identified as Sacred Sites and Power Places. Sacred Place(s) is the term used in this book to identify both.

The word sacred refers to an extraordinary or unique object, person or place of veneration and awe.

WHAT ARE SACRED SITES AND POWER PLACES?

SUNGATE, TIAHAUNACO, BOLIVIA

The idea of a Sacred Place…is apparently as old as life itself.
Joseph Campbell, *The Mythic Image*

Our senses tingle with a curiosity about what lies beyond this physical and visible world; what else exists that we cannot see. The Great Mystery, invisible worlds, ancient and future wisdom, and our intergalactic beginnings remain cloaked in mystery—yet each of us holds a unique piece of this intricate human puzzle.

The realm of Eternal Divine Self conveys a knowing of the existence of something larger than this life. A goddess, a god, religion, something to believe in, a faith, exceptional wisdom or a being more extraordinary than ourselves—all exist to nourish our need to aspire to something greater. Sacred Places have always been the locations and repositories for such yearnings.

Sacred Places allow spiritual communication—are human freeways to remembrance of our Eternal Divine Self.

These ancestral repositories hold a wealth of information about our hidden history, keys to our true nature that reveal pathways to our future as a species. Archaeology and history continue to revise ideas of the earliest civilizations based on new discoveries and evidence. I believe we are much older as a species, have been on the planet longer than our histories tell us and have created civilizations that are yet to be raised from the dust or the depths of the oceans.

Sacred Places are certainly part of our collective past and an esteemed part of our Eternal Now. Have you ever thought that your life may be happening in many different places and times, even simultaneously? Have you considered the possibility that our origins and the origins of Sacred Places are much deeper and older than archaeologists and historians assume from the evidence they uncover? Do you sense there is more going on beneath the surface? Have you ever visited a Sacred Place as a casual tourist and found yourself suddenly drawn to explore more deeply? Sacred Places are excellent locations to discover the answers to these deeper Life questions.

WHAT MAKES THEM SACRED?

The sacred stands apart from the norm and manifests itself
as a reality different from normal realities.

Sacred Places have the power to heal, inspire the mind, awaken, clarify, and support the development of psychic abilities. Archaeological sites are not all sacred and Sacred Places have varying levels of aliveness. Following is a description of the differences between Sacred Sites and Power Places.

SACRED SITES

Sacred Sites are places of religious or historical importance for indigenous people. A sacred site can also be a spot or location where a Sacred Person has visited, lived, performed miracles, said prayers upon or become enlightened. For instance, the Bodhi Tree where Buddha meditated and became enlightened was already a holy place. Buddha's enlightenment at that spot gave it another dimension of sacredness.

The appearance of the Blessed Virgin Mary at a cave in Lourdes, France is another example of a place that was already considered holy (the cave) being visited by a Sacred Person (Blessed Virgin Mary). The eighteen visions of Bernadeta Sobirós (now, Saint Bernadette), further evidenced the sacredness of the site.

Other Sacred Places upon the landscape may have forever been regarded as holy, showing evidence of continuous occupation or reverence from the earliest of times. Chartres Cathedral in France was previously a well that was a pilgrimage site and, before that, a Druid site. Civilizations continue to build Sacred Places atop those of the past.

It is often believed that Sacred Sites are the homes of gods or sacred beings.

Divination is often practiced at Sacred Sites, based on the idea that the gods or other powerful supernatural forces can reveal information and knowledge about the present and future. The Oracle at Delphi in Greece is an example of a sacred site specifically known for divination.

The ancient Greeks sited a shrine at Delphi to honor the earth Goddess Gaia. Their choice of location was not by chance...The sages asserted among other things that a mysterious substance called the "plenum" bubbled up from the ground there in abundance and that such an abundance favored Gaia and the work of the priestess oracle, Pithia, to prophesy... Modern psychology and design have tossed aside such ideas of places of power, but our bodies and minds still hear their call and respond to them.

James A. Swan, *The Power of Place and Human Environments*

POWER PLACES

Spiritual explorers (also called pilgrims) make power places their destinations, often inspired by the sacred ambiance or a mystical, magical energy. They feel a relationship to a place or make a journey based on a calling they receive to visit.

Many original or natural features and power places have been altered by man— like building a church over a sacred stone or rock. In these instances, the power place becomes inseparable from the structure built above it.

Grace Cathedral (in San Francisco) is sited on an ancient Indian Sacred Place marked by two artesian springs.

James A. Swan, *The Power of Place and Human Environments*

The Cathedral of Santo Domingo in Cusco, Peru is an example of such a place. Beneath the Christian structure is Kiswarkancha (today known as Qoricancha), the Inca palace of Viracocha, ruler of Cuzco. The Temple of the Sun stood as the center or navel of the world and remnants of it can be seen today inside and outside the cathedral. Some examples of Power Places are:

- where sky meets earth on top of a mountain or hill
- earth, sky, and water conjunct
- a major river rises from the earth
- where fire and water mix—a hot spring
- caves
- mountain passes
- confluences of ley lines

Besides auspicious geomantic features, great rocks (mountains, peaks), lakes and springs, confluences of water and sky and burial sites are often power places.

SACRED PLACES

Her citizens, imperial spirits, rule the present from the past.
Percy Bysshe Shelly, *Hellas*

We have established, built, named, and visited Sacred Places in every corner of the world since our arrival on the planet. In the past we were connected to nature—earth, sky and the elements. As natural seers—knowledge was intuitive, communication was telepathic, and energy could be seen and sensed. Places of exceptional earth energy were recognized, and we knew these places acted as gateways to higher realms. We instinctively knew the soul was nurtured and uplifted by visiting Sacred Places.

CAHOKAI SUNSET | | Painting by Luminous Antonio

Today, Sacred Places continue to send their magnetic vibrations across the planet, inviting us to visit. Books, online sites, magazines and visual media, rich with images and stories of places of antiquity and long-lost civilizations, inspire us and stir our curiosity. The Great Pyramid at Giza and The Sphinx in Egypt; Delphi, Greece, where the oracle spoke to sovereigns; the majestic mountaintop city of Machu Picchu in Peru; megalithic stone circles like Stonehenge and the Mayan pyramids of Central America are a few examples.

Now, as in ancient times, Sacred Places are powerful, vibrant transmitters and receptive beneficiaries of experience and wisdom. Records of the past and visions of the future reveal themselves intimately and personally to visitors who are open and sensitive to their messages.

> *At Sacred Places, the veils between the worlds are thin, even transparent.*
> *Those who normally do not see the people, places and things inhabiting*
> *invisible worlds have visions and revelatory dreams.*

Examples of a few of the best-known Sacred Places are listed below. This is a random list and in no way indicates these places have greater power or significance than any of the thousands of Sacred Places around the world. We may find the most simple, basic site to be powerful for us.

AUSTRALIA . . . . Uluru
CAMBODIA . . . . Angkor Wat
EGYPT . . . . Great Pyramid & Sphinx
ENGLAND . . . . .Stonehenge, Chalice Well, Avebury
GREECE . . . . .Delphi
GUATEMALA . . . . Tikal, Lake Atitlan, Quirigua
INDIA . . . . .Mahabodhi Temple, Kashi Vishwanath Temple, Varanasi
ITALY . . . . St. Peter's Basilica, Rome
MEXICO . . . . .Chichen Itza, Palenque, Tulum
PERU . . . . Machu Picchu, Qoricancha
SAUDI ARABIA . . . . .Kaaba, Mecca
TIBET . . . . Lhasa, Mt. Kailash
TOYKO . . . . Meiji Shrine
TURKEY . . . . Hagia Sofia, Gobekli Tepi
UNITED STATES . . . . Sedona, Cahokia Mounds, Chaco Canyon

PLACEMENT AND LOCATION

Every physical influence, including the frequency and vibration of the earth, designated the orientation and location of Sacred Places. The design of the structure or site was intended to enhance the consciousness and energy levels of visitors.

The sun, the moon and the stars dictated specific locations to capture the energy according to the seasons.

The King's chamber in the great pyramid at Giza, Glastonbury Tor in England and Sinagua and Anasazi sites in the Southwest, USA, are aligned with the constellation of Orion.

An example of a specific alignment can be seen at the temple Chichen Itza, in Yucatan, Mexico, where Kukulkan, the feathered serpent of Mayan lore, ascends the pyramid steps at the fall equinox and descends them in the spring—all through the movement of light. Tiahuanaco in Bolivia is aligned with the Winter Solstice. Stonehenge, England, is aligned with the summer solstice sunrise.

Solstice and equinox times are ideal for sacred rituals as the energy is strongest and can be directed toward connecting with higher realms, healing, or fertility.

The most powerful Sacred Places are those where you connect deeply and receive the most value.

LOCATING SACRED PLACES

Ancient civilizations hidden deep under nature's umbrella of green and jungle and beneath the ocean waters are now being located, with new technology bringing the distant past to light.

Here is a list of some of the ways ancient and pre-historic archaeological sites are located:

- Maps
- Historical documents
- Previous archaeological records
- Old tithe maps and terriers
- Legal records, wills, court records
- Pictorial records such photographs paintings, and engravings, and descriptive accounts written in books, diaries and travelogues.
- Myths, legends and stories of antiquity
- Visual surveys on foot
- Phosphate analysis.
- Geochemical surveying.
- Geophysical surveying (electrical resistively and magnetometry)
- Archaeology from space (NASA and Quick Bird satellites)
- Resistivity surveying – use of electrical currents.
- Ground Penetrating Radar (GPR) and Geographic Information Systems (GIS)
- Aerial photography
- Ancient books, manuscripts, cuneiform tablets, inscriptions in stone on clay tablets, leather documents and fragmentary texts on papyrus.
- Existing settlements are clues as cities and civilizations are often built one on top of the next. Archaeological sites buried beneath present day cities cannot be unearthed – Athens, Rome and Jerusalem are examples.
- The bible gives 6000 years of information including precise, exact locations of many raised and forgotten cities and once busy ports.

Below is a short overview by Dr. J.J. Hurtak explaining his field work regarding the world grid map of sacred places in his *The Keys of Enoch®*, a paraphysical textbook published in 1973.

"One of the principal themes of my archaeological research throughout the world has been the masterful interconnection between the sacred places of lost temples and pyramids once on the surface, but now underwater. One such place is under the ocean near the site of Yonaguni, Japan, and another is on land, buried beneath water under the Giza Plateau of Egypt, where the Shor Expedition, using radar, found 'The Tomb of Osiris' in 1997. My wife, Desiree, and I were principal team members and discoverers. (This was later announced to the world by the Egyptian Antiquities Department in 1999). These findings were based on my direct experience as written in my book The Keys of Enoch® in 1973 (Key 215), wherein I created a map of the sites that later was confirmed through scientific expeditions with archaeologists and geologists in Japan (University of Okinawa), Australia and the United States (Scripps Oceanographic Institute). The information on Japan was later released in a DVD called the Temple of Mu (IMD Films). In 1973, I described from this experience of mine, several key sacred locations both in the Far East and Near East, which are only two key areas of a larger grid/planetary vortex structure. To quote The Keys®, "...pyramids are uniquely positioned at key nodal points of the world grid which exists with the larger parent grid of Divine Evolution." All these pyramids around the world are part of a larger grid structure that is being activated by us today. Some areas are thousands of years old, but all, collectively, are important for the greater energy activation taking place at this time."

J.J. Hurtak, Ph.D. (U. of California), Ph.D. (U. of Minnesota), archaeologist, social scientist, futurist, author is the author of the important book, *The Book of Knowledge: The Keys of Enoch®*. Published by The Academy for Future Science and translated into twenty-five languages.

MANY TYPES OF SACRED PLACES

Sacred Places exist worldwide and in many forms. While ancient places are not all sacred, each place has a story to tell. Below are some examples of the different types of Sacred Places:

NATURAL SITES
Mountains, caves, unique natural features on the earth, forests, trees, groves, landscape carvings: Mt. Kailash, Tibet; Mt. Shasta, USA; San Francisco Peaks, Flagstaff, Arizona USA.

SACRED WATERS
Wells, springs, cenotes, rivers, lakes: Chalice Well, England; Montezuma's Well, Arizona, USA.

HOLY PLACES
Shrines, altars, places where relics are kept, birth and death places of saints, apparition sites, Marian sites, monasteries, tombs of saints, sanctuaries, places

where miracles have occurred, places where enlightenment has occurred, miracle working statues or icons: Potala Palace, Lhasa, Tibet; Our Lady of Guadalupe, Mexico.

STRUCTURES
Temples and cathedrals, pyramids, ruins: Luxor Temple, Egypt; Tikal, Guatemala; Copan, Honduras.

EARTHWORKS
Labyrinths, medicine wheels, megalithic-chambered mounds and earth mounds, standing stones, landscape carvings: Bighorn Medicine Wheel, USA; Cahokia Mounds, Illinois USA; Carnac, France; Newgrange, Ireland.

UNIQUE LOCATIONS
Creation story locations and boundaries, burial sites, Sacred Portals recounting star migration (past and present), places of prehistoric revelation, spirit sites, locations of mythological importance, ceremonial sites, places chosen by animals or birds, astronomical observatories, stones of healing and power, oracular sites, places of attained enlightenment, places of emergence, dragon sightings and slayings. Sacred islands and places chosen by divinatory methods like dowsing: Mahabodhi Temple, India; Doorway of Amara Meru, Lake Titicaca, Peru; Delphi, Greece; Monte Alban, Mexico. Peru; Delphi, Greece; Monte Alban, Mexico.

ANCESTRAL PLACES
Archaeological sites, pueblos, cliff dwellings, kivas are but a few places of the ancestors. In essence, any place on the earth where people gathered and lived are places of our ancestors.

TOMBS
Houses, in many prehistoric cultures, were the earliest tombs with the dead buried in their own home complete with whatever it was determined might be needed in the afterlife. Tombs are dwellings to protect the dead and provide them with necessities for their next adventure.

Later, Stone Age tombs were shaped like houses, with two large vertical stones and another stone slab laid horizontally across them as the "roof." They too, were filled with tools, food and personal possessions necessary for the next life.

Some of the most famous tombs in the world include the pyramids of Egypt, the Taj Mahal, Thirteen Tombs of the Ming Dynasty, Church of the Holy Sepulcher and the Prophet's Mosque in Medina.

The monumental Great Pyramid in Egypt may be the most remarkable example; however, no remains have been found in any of the areas noted as tombs and the use for these areas may have been other than burial.

We stand on hallowed ground at the grave or tomb, the last physical reminder or marker bespeaking the existence of a person. When visiting a tomb, we honor the memory and accomplishments of the person. Contemplation and prayer may connect us with the essence of their lives initiating a visceral sense, stirring memories and insights of within us.

During 2002, I took a group of six women on an adventure in a van exploring the Yucatan Peninsula to see as many of the archaeological sites as possible. We started with Coba, Tulum and visited several smaller sites before we reached our ultimate destination, Palenque. Then we travelled up to Merida and visited Chichen Itza, Kabah, Uxmal and every other site in that area. All along the way we were stopped by the military who asked a few questions in Spanish and allowed us to move on. We slowed for the inevitable speed bumps (topos) present in every small village along the way.

TEMPLE OF INSCRIPTIONS, CHIAPAS, MEXICO

We remained at Palenque for a few ridiculously hot and humid days and the highlight was gaining access to Pakal's Tomb inside the Pyramid of Inscriptions. A letter had to be written in Spanish explaining the reason we were applying for admission to the tomb of Pakal the Great. As "archaeology students", we gained access.

The steps down into the center of the pyramid were tall and wet; the humidity was stifling. I remember reading it took four years to clear the rubble on these steps leading to the tomb. It was a rite of passage just to make one's way down and

STAIRCASE TO PAKAL'S TOMB, TEMPLE OF INSCRIPTIONS, CHIAPAS, MEXICO

then at the very bottom, in a small room that only fit a couple people at a time, you could view the famous tomb.

I thought about how the priests, long after Pakal's passing, listened for his ongoing messages and sage advice through a tube that extended from his tomb to the top of the pyramid. The essence and presence of Pakal stayed with me and is still with me today.

PAKALS MASK, PAKAL'S TOMB, TEMPLE OF INSCRIPTIONS, CHIAPAS, MEXICO*

PALENQUE

mangoes crash to the ground
splatting and splashing their juicy sweetness onto the earth
a rich jungle canopy shields the bodies
of screaming howler monkeys
while silent jaguars circle from habit

clothed in long white tunics
dark silky haired--rainforest dwelling
guardians of jungle ruins
Yaxchilan and Bonampak
where it is said the gods resided
when they lived on earth

ancient Lancandon Maya
who conquistadors never found
appear at the entry portal to Palenque, Chiapas, Mexico
place of serpents-realm of the jaguar
Palenque's Temple of Inscriptions
carved into the lush steaming jungle
climb a path and jump to an upper ledge
walk to the front-up steps to the top
slip through a black net hanging at the entry
protecting the temple from birds and bats

inside-an opening in the floor
to a steep limestone staircase
slick with moisture
frozen in time
steps more suited for giants than humans
heavy wet air slippery with Atlantean pearls
studded emeralds of knowledge
invisibly incised into the walls

at the bottom-behind a metal grate
the tomb of one who
from the stars came
ancient Mayan ruler
alien airline pilot-tunnel car traveler
Pacal Votan-Pacal the Great

in 1939 almost 1300 years later
Dr. Jose Arguelles is born
world renowned visionary, educator, author of

The Mayan Factor
Earth Ascending

The Call of Pacal Votan
an originator of Earth Day
initiator of the 1987 harmonic convergence
sparks massive renewed interest in Sacred Places around the world

Arguelles invokes
star people, ancestors, extra terestrials, extra higher dimensionals
above-crystalline earth
below-another earth within this earth
that knows us-but we know it not
reminding us
it is between these intelligences we live

he says
we cannot survive the mistake of living in artificial time
out of harmony with the universe
indigenous people are the caretakers of the biosphere
and a whole a new society
will evolve indigenous values
into new
galactic
cultural forms
to be shared by all people as one-on Earth.

supernovas sending out cosmic messages
Pacal Votan says-Jose Arguelles says
return to natural time
avoid
dodge and redirect
override
reverse
stop in its tracks
biospheric destruction

lead a simpler life
communicate telepathically
breathe with the heartbeat of the earth

lead a simpler life
communicate telepathically
breathe with the heartbeat of the earth

Luminous Antonio, 2002

3

WHY WE VISIT
SACRED PLACES

DOORWAY TO FAMARA MERU, LAKE TITICACA, PERU

WHY WE VISIT SACRED PLACES

TA PROHM TEMPLE, ANGKOR WAT

There is a record of Sacred Places written on our soul and incised on our bones—a song, imprinted on our DNA and flowing through us like the blood that feeds our body.

To visit a Sacred Place is a calling—a desire to renew a connection or a knowing that there is something a place has to impart to us. We are not alone in these inclinations. We have been anointed with the elixir of deep soul memory, demanding our presence at locations near and far. Many of us will travel to Sacred Places to restore our multi-dimensional being self to wholeness—to surrender any limitations and reconnect with the Eternal Divine Self.

Our multi-sensory system is tuned to specific vibrations and frequencies. We contact and connect with those beings and events present on our frequency and timeline.

On a multidimensional clock or calendar, our arrival has been awaited and we are honored guests carrying valuable information and insights in our energy fields. Visiting Sacred Places broadens our perspective and rearranges our priorities. We see ourselves more clearly, helping us to define our purpose.

> *Sacred Places trigger memories of our Eternal Divine*
> *Self bring clarity and reveal our next steps.*

These mysterious ancient places awaken, inspire, heal, catalyze and gracefully instill the qualities of wisdom, compassion, peace of mind and insight in those who visit. Many cannot describe their reasons for wanting to visit a Sacred Place. Afterwards, it may be difficult to describe exactly what happened. Inevitably, a great shift or change takes place—one that is often beyond words.

The magic of Sacred Places is reflected in myths and legends that speak of healing, enlightenment, increased creativity, amplified psychic abilities, clarity and a heightened sense of Self and purpose.

BENEFITS OF THE JOURNEY

> *The most beautiful thing we can experience is the mysterious. It is the source of all true art and all science. He to whom this emotion is a stranger, who can no longer pause to wonder and stand rapt in awe, is as good as dead: his eyes are closed.* Albert Einstein

The journey you choose to make to a Sacred Place may challenge you spiritually, physically, emotionally and psychologically. This is all part of the matrix of change. Why make such a journey? What are the potential benefits one might expect to receive from visiting a Sacred Place? Identify any expectations for the changes that might transpire. Become aware of any intentions you may have for the journey.

> *When we visit Sacred Sites, we go there with humility, perform our acts of respect and then see what happens—we surrender to the place rather than try to 'control' it.*
> James Swan, *Sacred Places, How the Living Earth Seeks Our Friendship*

It is good to remember that this is a two-way street. Humans are also sacred fonts and vessels of information that the consciousness of our planet seeks. The effort we take to journey upon her surface is abundantly rewarded. Here are a few of the potential benefits of visiting Sacred Places:

- Receiving a vision illuminating a course or mission to pursue.

- Gives life new significance.

- Completing a journey to a Sacred Place instills confidence in our abilities and strength.

- Real or imagined limitations are transcended when we survive the journey.

- Discover additional sources of power beyond yourself.

- Enhance our link to humanity.

- Receive inner revelations and profound meaning for the direction of our life.

- Develop a deeper connection with ourselves, the natural world, society, and the soul.

- A deep connection with nature promotes understanding of ourselves as an organic part of the process.

- Deep realization that nature is our home–breathtakingly beautiful, nurturing and vibrantly alive.

- Learn to allow our Eternal Divine Self to take the lead and inform decisions.

- Develop a stronger appreciation for our friends and relations

- Renewed appreciation for life and material comforts.

- Release illusions.

- Learn to rely upon ourselves as our own source of wisdom rather than looking outward for answers (teachers, books, churches, gurus).

- Establish a deeper connection to the mystical and mythological aspects of life.

- Receive a new direction, foundation in life, self-definition, and values.

- Become familiar with the ancestors, spirits and guardians present in other dimensions.

- Receive answers to life's questions.

- Awaken to the truth.

Our finely tuned sensitivity and awareness is an accurate indicator of all changes—subtle or easily observable—physical, emotional, mental, and spiritual.

My third time in Egypt was 1996 where we entered the Great Pyramid with a private group. We laid on the floor with lights turned off, got inside the sarcophagus, harmonized the "omm" sound and meditated. I laid down on the floor and within seconds I was gone, thinking,

"How could I fall asleep so fast?"

The thought came, "Where am I?"and I heard,

"Do you care?"

My response was "No."

I went so far so quickly and had no idea where I was. I heard friends calling my name three times and that brought me back into my body. I noticed a red line going up the inside of my arms and legs and thought I was bit by something. I was told it was the completion of an initiation and that rang true. I also understood I was to become a joy magnet.

Not long after, my husband Gary had open heart surgery and I believe this initiation allowed me to stay very present and hold the light throughout this time.

I savored the experience and went back every year for 24 years, entered the Great Pyramid with my group for a private hour, meditated, harmonized the "omm" sound, laid on the floor. I carried a level of anticipation, thinking, hoping, wondering if something else would happen. Nothing ever did.

In January 2020 I went back in again, by now conditioned to expect nothing. As I laid down on the floor, I felt something circling the top of my head and thought,

"There must be a fan blowing on me." Then I remembered, there are no fans in here.

Again, I asked, "What is it?"

"...Do you care?"

"Not really."

My pillar of light 9 or 10 inches around entered through top of head and passed through my body all the way down to my feet. I could not move or think. Once the lights got turned on in the room, I realized this was another initiation and I was filled with light. I came out of this experience clear and centered, light-filled, and peaceful. It is hard to put into words, but I felt like I was emotionally lighter.

Soon after, I realized my phone had stopped working. What I did not know initially was I would be disconnected for month from friends and family. Phone numbers and contact information were all on the non-working phone. Even when I returned home, a series of events made replacing the phone problematic. I was already practicing isolation before the pandemic.

I believe the great pyramid is completely charged and I am amazed it took 25 year for the next experience. Many secrets of our pasts are available there.

Andrea Smith, Artist

Up On Magdalene's Mountain

A healer on the brink of closing my private practice, for 20 years I have had debilitating chronic fatigue syndrome. Doctors say there is no cure. Chronic – Chronos, that's time; Fatigue – army pants. OK. So I have "drill sergeant doing time in my body syndrome", sucking the soul right out of me.

I vow – no more meetings with remarkable men, no more juicing and chanting and visualizing. I do what my intuition tells me this time. In May of 1996, I fly to the south of France to climb, by myself, with the little energy I have left -up the sacred mountain to the pilgrimage site of Mary Magdalene's cave. My feet crunch on limestone, and I jump, nearly stepping on a garter snake as my ancestors rattle their chains inside my bones. I think of the curses of Eve, the matrix in my DNA that dissociates and suppresses my pure soul and forces me to live by mind and will alone, forever seeking acceptance for my unlovable, unforgivable self.

In painterly light the color of champagne, I vow to end to this inner division of body and soul, this   energy crisis of planetary proportion. I want the stolen returned, the suppressed to be released, because God dammit, I'm a mermaid. My name comes from Mer, for the ocean of creation from which all life comes- and from which all Mary's have received their walking papers: to live, serving the highest light within them.

I feel a déjà vu – the energy of Magdalene – as I ascend the sacred mountain. She knew The Way. The power inside me to be expansive, loving- and a blissful, erotic energy- begins moving inside my body. A liquid fire is rising from my feet up into the magnet of my heart. A radiant center has flown open, free of time and effort and will. Free to be in ease and grace. I have not lived this Way before.

Fairly flying up the mountain now, I arrive as two doves alight on the entrance to Magdalene's cave. On an ancient site of Isis, turned Catholic now, I kneel before an altar ablaze with hundreds of candles. Closing my eyes, I drift into the darkness of inner space, where Magdalene appears. Robed in light, eyes luminous with the cosmos itself, she points to her heart, the sacred heart, encircled with a crown of thorns.

"Because you have called me, I will show you The Way. First you must purify your self of all sorrow, anger, and expectation. These feelings are trapped in the cells of your body and soul. These are the source of your sickness. First, you must forgive yourself, and all the others, for their disconnection from love, causing violence. Seek to understand, not to be understood. Then, open this point in your heart where The Compassion of God's grace eternally flows to you, and receive it! Realize not for an instant are you separate from one molecule of the divine. Here within you, among the flowing fields of joy, is your true Self, the sacred flame of divine Presence of Source, God-being-You, and all the power of creation. Learn to direct it with your thought and feeling and it will bring you everything you need. As it has now done, for you have called it forth. This is the sacred law."

As Magdalene touched me between my eyebrows, a searing white light in the cave of my brain opened my third eye, re-connecting the bridge between heaven and earth. As Magdalene's form faded back into the formless, my body re-membered the divine physiology of our original Wholeness, our true origins as God's Light and Love. As the song "Ave Maria" floated up the mountain from the nun's singing their vespers in the village below, I emptied my bottles of pills and threw them off the mountain. Because Spirit creates matter, and what we deem miracles, when I arrive back to the states, my doctors are amazed. I am, in fact, bloody, merry well. This time I won't forget it.

Maureen Riley, Certified Master Healer and Intuitive Consultant

CEREMONIAL PRAYER*

4

WHEN TO VISIT SACRED PLACES

ANGKOR WAT PASSAGEWAY, CAMBODIA

WHEN TO VISIT SACRED PLACES

CHATH PUJA, THE FESTIVAL TO WORSHIP THE SUN GOD, INDIA*

Traditional religious people often visit sites tied to the history of their religion. Pilgrimages (e.g., Santiago de Compostela) may happen all at once or over several years. Buddhists may choose to visit the places that Buddha is known to have visited. Christians may be attracted to the places of miracles, like Lourdes in France, Jews, to the Temple Mount and Muslims to Mecca. Other religious groups may seek out those sites of historical and religious significance to them— temples, cathedrals, and shrines.

Many Sacred Places have been set up to highlight Equinox and Solstice times. Dates of festivals, ceremonies, religious holidays, and celebrations are also popular travel times. Spiritual explorers appear to have an internal clock indicating when it is time to visit. Inner knowing often catalyzes our journeys. We hear the call.

THE CALL

Being sensitive to when we are called to a site requires trust, a trust in our higher Self. This aspect of us is the catalyst, and at the time it can feel as though the urge to go someplace came out of the blue.

Generally, however, there are usually some early signs. For example, and often, there is some attraction to an area; we read something, know of a specific journey, are drawn to images in magazines and movies or the mention of a place keeps appearing in conversation. We can choose to pay attention to these signals, or not.

We may have an awareness of a past life, historical connection, wisdom teaching, or strong interest drawing us to visit a Sacred Place. There are times we just go and find out later what the draw was all about. Use the following exercise to determine whether a place and time is right for you:

Use the Spiritual Energy Expansion Nucleus (SEEN) outlined in the next section of this book to relax, center, and focus inward.

- Concentrate on an image of the destination you have in mind.
- With the image in place, see the proposed date of travel printed on the lower edge of the image.
- Imagine yourself in the picture—walking, sitting, exploring.
- Notice how you feel and how your body responds to being in the location of your inquiry.
- Ask if the guardians and the Sacred Place(s) are ready to receive you currently.
- Tune into and scan your body for signals and feelings.
- If a feeling is less than positive and uplifting, follow through by asking what the feeling is about.
- Come to completion with your process of looking inward.
- Write down what you have discovered.

You can also simply choose a place and time that appeals to you and go. One thing leads to another and you will find yourself on the journey of a lifetime.

"In the summer of 2007, I suddenly developed a fascination for crop circles. Even though I was living in New York City, I was inexplicably drawn to the new formations in Wiltshire fields, England.

After a few days of pouring over website after website dedicated to crop circles, I decided to fly to the U.K. I hired a car and randomly drove down to where the most crop circles were appearing. En route, I came across a small village called Pewsey in Wiltshire. So, I decided to stop there.

I went to a local bed and breakfast hotel but was told there were no rooms available. However, the proprietor informed me that another cottage nearby was open to guests. "It's not usual as it's a private home, but the person wants to rent a room out this summer," she told me.

The venue was an old 16th century dairy farm and I immediately felt that I was in the right place at the right time. That night, I slept solidly for 8-hours under a quaint thatched roof and timbered walls. Then, something odd happened.

To this day, I really can't recall what, but when I woke up, I just knew where to drive and which farmer's field to enter. The field contained a crop circle and I walked to the middle of it. Once still, I experienced a massive spike of electricity soaring up my spine from my feet which were firmly planted to the ground. I closed my eyes and then my arms immediately shot out-stretched at right angles on either side of my body. A few minutes passed that felt like several lifetimes and afterward, I felt completely altered. Next, I drove to the Avebury stone circle and spent the afternoon walking about its center.

When I got back to the States, I felt impelled to visit a local esoteric bookshop. There, a book about Star Gates and Ley Lines drew my attention. I thumbed toward the back of the book and discovered a map of Star Gates. That map revealed a Star Gate that was in a small village called Pewsey in rural England. It was the village I had stayed in.

Instantly, I was projected back to a far distant time when that part of England was covered in illuminated temple complexes and to a life I once had. It was as if a vital part of the puzzle had been put back. From that moment my life has massively shifted. A Sacred Place had called to me." Jacalyn Burke

Jacalyn's experience of being summoned to a certain location in England, and her heeding that call without hesitation, indicates that we are not talking about a phenomenon the rational mind can fathom.

CHOOSE YOUR TIME

Choices about times of day and season to visit a Sacred Place can be based on comfort and quiet. Whenever possible, avoid fighting the elements (cold, rain, intense heat) and the crowds. In a hotter climate, choose early morning or late afternoon; in cooler climates, choose afternoons when the sun is at its zenith, providing maximum warmth.

Do you really want to be at a Sacred Place with thousands of people? Maybe you do! Possibly there will be no choice in the matter. Consider your personality and how you might best enjoy your time at Sacred Places.

Seek the most peaceful and quiet moments when the fewest number of people are around, and the crowds have left or not yet arrived. Locate a quiet, less visited area of the site. Undisturbed, you can connect with nature and the earth and enjoy the subtle sounds of animals, birds, or the wind in the trees.

5

WHAT HAPPENS AT SACRED PLACES?

TEMPLE OF THE MOON, QUILLARUMIYOQ, PERU

WHAT HAPPENS AT SACRED PLACES?

OFFERING PUJA FLOWERS, GANGES RIVER, VARANASI, INDIA*

Swirling smoky trails of incense and sounds of chanting and drumming may have filled the air for hundreds or thousands of years before our arrival. We become part of an ongoing ceremony as our feet touch the earth and we walk through Sacred Places.

Sacred Places hold many keys to the nature, cycles and unfolding of our lives. When we visit Sacred Places, we can sense in new and different ways and we know on a very deep level that something has shifted or clarified within us. While we may not be able to measure what happens in a scientific way, we sense that hidden dimensions beyond our range of normal sight are operating.

Since all matter is condensed light, light is the source, the cause of life. Therefore, light is divine. The flowers have a direct line to God that an evangelist would kill for. Tom Robbins

We enter the energy field of a site when we arrive in the immediate area. The energy field of a Sacred Place is teeming with information that saturates the natural elements (earth, stones, waters, trees, plants) and structures at the location. As we walk through a site in the third dimension, we pass by and through mystical doorways reaching far into the past and future. Our energy field connects with the fields of the site, exchanging and sharing information and possibilities in much the same way we do when we meet with a friend, associate, mentor or lover.

Each conscious footstep we take at a Sacred Place is a merging of spirit —human, trees, rocks, air, animals, ancestors, wind, sky, water, the beings of the earth upon which we walk. A nonstop stream of information flows to us and through us as the information we carry is shared in return.

A transference of energy takes place between Sacred Places and the visitor. As visitors to these sites, we record our impressions with video, photography, or audio devices. We point a camera in the direction of a specific doorway or rock formation, hoping to capture something that can be felt rather than seen. Simultaneously, the earth records impressions of our visits, our energy and the record of our soul remains in the energy field of the site. Our presence at Sacred Places is valuable.

Phenomena occurring at Sacred Places are produced by the cumulative experience of all who have visited and the events that have occurred—all is retained in the energy field of the site itself.

Sacred Places and specific locations within the site are encircled by distinct and information-rich fields of energy.

The specific orientation or location of Sacred Places allows for a steady stream of life force to emanate from them. Celestial and earthly alignments are calculated to enhance our lives, charge our energy, heal and revitalize our bodies. Ongoing visits and intentions for Sacred Places keep them alive.

The scalp prickles when we pass a certain ancient doorway; we shiver, spine-chilled, in such a spot as the ceremonial cavern at Bandelier; the voice drops to a whisper at Chartres...
D.M. Dooling, "Focus," *Parabola 3*, issue 1, 1978

The influence of the stars beaming spiritual energy onto the earth, the matrix of ley lines (read: *Ley Lines and Earth Energies*, David Cowan and Chris Arnold) crisscrossing the planet and connecting Sacred Places, myths, and legends, telling of the alchemy of times past, all leave their indelible imprint.

We are catalyzed onward in our life's journey; we gain greater clarity and make better decisions; we release the past and make way for the new; we see ourselves and the world in a different way. This invisible yet palpable power refreshes and stabilizes us.

Everything is significant when we are at a Sacred Place. The presence of an animal brings messages and teachings to us. The flight of an eagle may remind us to choose a higher perspective, since the eagle flies higher than any other bird. The snake that sheds its skin by crawling out of it may appear to remind us that we are in a cycle of transformation, shedding the old (skin).

We may not understand the song the bird sings, but we can be certain that the vibration of its song feeds into our field and is sent as a loving and healing gift.

Stones, mountains, waters or whatever a site holds also send out a song (vibration), although silent in most cases.

We meet ourselves on a deeper level at Sacred Places. Much as a student can learn from a meeting with a great master, we access greater wisdom within ourselves during these journeys.

When we are at the site, engrossed in the moment, it is not always possible to decipher the messages we are receiving. Signals and vibrations broadcasting into our energy field often wait for translation later. We receive messages that are uniquely ours. There is no right way to receive a message or to interpret it. You are the master interpreter.

INVISIBLE WORLDS

Perceiving, accessing, and interacting with all levels of creation is our human destiny.

Through our eyes we see only five per cent of the world around us, unaware of the matrix connecting all life; blind to the multidimensional worlds and beings that surround us. We are multidimensional beings living in a multidimensional universe—spirit in the material world, in a physical body.

When we choose to allow our full perceptive abilities to operate, we gain access to multidimensional reality, the realm of spirit and cumulative knowledge of those who came before.

Levels of life beyond linear time, eclipsed from our ordinary vision, are the domain of shamans, seers, mystics and medicine people who regularly commune with the world of spirit and delve into the unseen and invisible. They perceive all matter as alive, as living energy. Sacred Places are vibrantly alive and one of the living realms of spirit.

Silence is a powerful practice supporting our dialogue and connection with the unseen.

People in cultures around the world honor their ancestors. Altars are kept and offerings are made to those who live in other dimensions. Multidimensional reality is integrated as part of life and the beings that inhabit it are known and honored.

Indigenous cultures recognize the gods or the sacred energy of rivers, stones, mountains, earth, streams, animals and all elements of nature.

The fact that we have been disconnected from the natural world and rhythms of the universe for so long does not foretell a permanent condition.

We are conditioned to perceive the world in a linear manner and to use our five senses and logical mind as the main information sources. What is known as extrasensory perception is destined to become the new normal.

Interaction with Sacred Places requires a willingness to enter the realm of spirit. Our innate multi-sensory system connects us with invisible worlds.

laws of physics:
invisible, eternal, omnipresent, all powerful
trust, we must, if we are to survive
creating worlds of magic and miracles
strong in our lives

100 billion galaxies spin and whirl through the universe
our limited sight sees only five
like ants we scurry busy with what we can see and do
blind to what makes it all work

everything of importance is invisible to us and we take it for granted
stars, unseen by day glow brilliantly in the night sky
transparent cosmic glue holds the universe of stars and planets together
while filaments and cords of gravity somehow sustain our earthly walk

a kiss, time, the future, atoms, gas and radio waves are all beyond our range of sight
light is unseen to us without the opposite of darkness
we learn that the horizon does not exist as we move toward it

and who has ever found the end of a rainbow
not knowing how electricity works we continue to rely upon it

art is the misinterpreted signature of the invisible

Luminous Antonio, 2008

EXPECT THE UNEXPECTED

*If the doors of perception were cleansed, everything would
appear to man as it is, infinite.* William Blake

Journeys to Sacred Places provide an opportunity to step into dimensions and realities that differ from what we are accustomed to in our everyday life. It is important to be sensitive to ourselves, others, and the delicate environments we explore. The more sensitivity we can practice, the richer our experience will be.

Drop any expectations—leave them behind. Taking the time to be informed has great value, and you may find all you have read, heard, or thought about a Sacred Place is about to be shown as inadequate or simply wrong.

*When we are truly open and sensitive, our experience is unlikely to match our
expectations. The unexpected meeting, situation, realization, or vision is a teller of
truths. Be observant and receptive.*

TIMELESSNESS

*In the stillness of your presence, you can feel your own formless and timeless reality as
the unmanifested life that animates your physical form. You can then feel the same life
deep within every other human and every other creature. You look beyond the veil of
form and separation. This is the realization of oneness. This is love.* Eckhart Tolle

Timelessness can be perfectly defined in the kiss.

We have all, at one time or another, unconsciously slipped between time. It may have been on those long hot summer afternoons when we played as children with the neighborhood kids. What had felt like an hour was in fact many hours later, for which we were scolded by our worried parents.

Or perhaps it was in the moment we locked eyes with the love of our life across a crowded room, and time stood still. It may have been in the moments we held our first-born and everything in the universe appeared to a halt. In such sublime occurrences we have effortlessly managed to stop time.

But we can also, consciously, appear to manipulate time such as when we step into multidimensional realities at Sacred Places—a realm where time does not exist. Ideas of good, bad, right, or wrong are also nonexistent. Here, we expertly reach through the veils of illusion and vastness of experience and wisdom to find the exact information, remedies, balms, answers, and visions for the Ever-present Eternal Now.

WHAT YOU SEE IS WHAT YOU GET

There is no fixed reality here.

It was late afternoon on an overcast August day, and I was the guide for three spiritual explorers in Sedona, Arizona. We were driving down a dirt road going toward a place in the desert for a fire ceremony.

A woman in the back seat called out, "Look, a cat." I stopped the car and from the left side came a wild cat who crossed in front of the car and bounded up the embankment on the right and on into the desert. It happened in an instant and I was amazed at what I saw. Living here for over twenty years, I had never seen a wild cat.

It was a couple days later while talking to a friend when it occurred to me that we might have, as people often do, seen different things. I emailed the other people who were in the car asking them to tell me what they saw.

The woman who spotted the cat and called out to us saw a "tan or light brown colored fur, no markings. The cat weighed about thirty pounds."

Another woman saw "a thickly furred, medium sized feline with a graceful power to its stride and a curious gaze. Its fur was dappled with dark spots and bands, while most of it was the color of sand, only with more of a caramel tone to it. The tail was a black stub and it seemed to have pointed ears with long fur rising from them. It looked to weigh about fifty pounds."

The man saw "a large tan cat weighing in at around a hundred pounds."

I saw a cat of approximately 4-5 feet in length from head to tail that weighed at least 80 pounds, maybe more. The cat was bright golden orange with black spots, rosettes, and stripes at the hindquarter. For me, it had an electric brilliance to the colors—it appeared to be a jaguar.

Whatever you see and experience is meant specifically for you and is to be trusted completely. It may not be what others see, even if they are standing right next to you. Two people standing in the same place at the same time, looking at the same thing, see and experience differently. This is one way we recognize the distortions of history, his story. His story is only one viewpoint, not necessarily the one we may want to embrace as truth.

As Integrative Archaeologists, we rely upon and trust
our own insights and information—fully.

There is no right or wrong, better, or worse, good or bad, there is simply what is for each of us. Our perception defines our reality experience. Trusting what we see gives each of us accurate information.

SARCOPHOGUS | Painting by Luminous Antonio

AM I HEARING THINGS?

Our clairaudient abilities come alive at Sacred Places. It is not unusual to hear a word shouted out, or a name, or other information. Directions like "stop," "go left," "sit down" are more easily heard at Sacred Places. Words or phrases may come into your head—listen. Don't judge it, listen and be willing to open to more information. Always trust the information you receive.

AM I SEEING THINGS?

Did the rocks suddenly show me a picture of something or someone? Did I imagine that rock just became transparent and I could see inside? Did someone walk into the shadows in the back of that temple? Our abilities to see the invisible world are greatly enhanced at Sacred Places. Take note, pay attention, and allow the images or visions to emerge.

We are driving across a baron stretch of road in the Southwest when I, the passenger, say "I need a bathroom."
"The next town is 50 miles away." I hear from my friend. I know that, but I still need a bathroom.

Stark landscape unfolds left and right, behind, and ahead, and I am scanning around for a bush or tree or rock I can crouch behind and release the contents of my bladder. There is nothing in sight and pressure builds; ten minutes pass and we continue to drive.

I am looking hard for something that does not exist.

Wavy air like what you see across a hot desert up ahead, distorts the road and land in the distance. Suddenly, my friend is laughing as he says, "I may be wrong, but it looks like a port-a-john out in the middle of the desert!" He points off to the left "you are an amazing manifestor!"

I can't believe my eyes, as we draw closer, I see it is exactly that …a portable bathroom neatly placed on the side of the road. There is no road work, construction, building, no nothing going on out here! We drive over and I rush to open the door to what is a completely, brand new, apparently never been used, portable bathroom. The toilet paper is even folded in a V at the end like you find when you check into a hotel.

I am grateful. The universe is kind. Still, as we drive away, I look back to see if the big blue box in the middle of the desert remains and I track it till the road turns and it slips from sight.

THOUGHTS ARE CLUES

Notice your thoughts and follow them through. Does the thought you are thinking have anything to do with the place you are standing, the event that just occurred or words that were just spoken?

SEE THE OTHER SIDE

If you have always thought things were one way, you may find reversals on your journey. Discoveries we make as Integrative Archaeologists often present a whole new side of life. Be willing to accept that things may be quite different from how you previously perceived them.

SELF AS SACRED PLACE

The study of mysteries requires courage and a willingness to participate in a powerful adventure of the soul that is at once both universal and intensely personal. Jean Houston

Our travels to Sacred Places are a lens through which we view, examine, and come to know more about the Sacred Place closest to home—our Self. As spirits in the material world, we inhabit a physical body, a temple and sanctuary supporting the indwelling sacredness of life itself. Each of us has written on our soul the wisdom of all times, the magic and miracles dreamed and performed, the absolute heights to which humanity has aspired and all our achievements during our long earthly walk.

As sacred and divine beings we have the inherent abilities to know, change, heal and transform anything. Choosing to live life in the natural flow of the universe is one key to experiencing the magic of life.

I am a trusting leaf being carried along on the stream of life.

Places of peaceful refuge, (i.e. a garden, a special walk, or a meditation space) restore, replenish and renew us for the journey through life. Visiting Sacred Places located away from home shifts the matrix of day-to-day life initiating a revitalizing effect as multidimensional aspects of our being are revealed. Can we sit in a sacred space at home and simultaneously visit a sacred site? Yes, absolutely!

We have within us everything necessary to project our
consciousness anywhere in this world or beyond.

Each of us is a Sacred Place to be honored, respected, revered and loved. Our journey through this life and the experiences we create lead us to the Eternal Divine Self, who we really are. We are Sacred Places, each of us—godlike beings.

As we reclaim the Eternal Divine Self, we initiate and sustain the highly
desirable effect of overriding the limitations present in consensus reality.

RED TEMPLE IN ASIA | Painting by Luminous Antonio

6

THE INFLUENCE OF MYTHOLOGY

BIRTH OF VENUS, PAINTING BY BOTTICELLI

THE INFLUENCE OF
MYTHOLOGY

Obscured by the veils of time, myths have been erroneously mislaid in the realm of fable, invention, fantasy, or simple fiction. Ancient myths echo from times long gone, are translated from languages since forgotten and speak of worlds that have become invisible. The beings, places and events inhabiting these old stories seem unbelievable to us in modern times. Myths hail from beyond this world, at the time of beginnings and speak of what we see as mystical or supernatural experience.

As fantastic as it may seem, it is likely that myths simply state the way it was.

PICTOGRAPH, SOUTHWEST, USA | Painting by Luminous Antonio

The heroes and superhuman beings we meet in myths display their Sacred Powers to model behaviors, morals, and the meanings of life for us. We interpret what we cannot understand, personally experience, or see as the actions of supernatural, superhuman beings, as the acts of gods.

These gods were often tied to Sacred Places (i.e. Cave of Zeus in Greece). King Arthur of the Round Table and his knights (Glastonbury, England); Arjuna and Krishna of the *Bhagavad-Gita* (Cave of Arjuna); the Homeric epics (Crete, Greek island of the Gods) and the Sumerian Gilgamesh (Garden of the gods) are a few examples of great and enduring stories. These stories give us insights into different cultures, times, traditions, and outlooks, expanding our view of the world, possibilities, and ourselves.

Myths and legends are passed down through oral traditions, from generation to generation, providing answers to the basic questions of life:

- Who am I?
- Why am I here?
- What is my purpose?
- What is my role?
- How do I fit into the human and natural world?
- How should I live?

A myth can assist us on our walk-through life, giving us a sense of what our journey is about and how others have prevailed against similar challenges.

Our human journey is translated into cosmological terms through myths. Every myth and legend will offer some truth and when our hearts open, we see and hear the story beneath the myth and feel it is spoken directly to us, about us, and for us.

It is always wise to reap the benefits of the lessons from those who have already walked the paths we find ourselves upon. Integrative Archaeologists often consider myths in their explorations, seeing clearly and personally what value a myth may hold. A great story, like a great piece of art, allows the viewer total freedom of interpretation. In this way, each person can see their own story revealed, their beliefs out pictures and their challenges made clear.

We play a variety of roles at different times in our lives and so our role within a myth will change as well. We may embody or embrace the characteristics of Athena and go on to integrate Venus or Isis. It is not as if one myth will guide us for a lifetime. If we are committed to change, we are likely to pass through many characters and stories, each holding a piece of the great mystery and the saga of our lives.

In the distant past, the gods made their presence known and were not strictly consigned to heaven or some invisible place—they were seen and heard. Animals, people, stones, mountains, rivers, streams, buildings and even time itself was held as sacred and each one had a voice.

Sacred Places located around the world are dignified as sacred due to events that have taken place in the past—and continue to take place today. The reason supernatural and paranormal aspects of Sacred Places have continued to attract visitors is partially due to myths and legends, large and small, continuously recited up to this day. Stories are passed from people who visit the sites, to other people who may not have yet done so. We are the modern-day makers and performers of the new myths and legends.

KING MINOS MYTH

A long, long time ago (even for the ancient Greeks) there lived a demi-god King called Minos who reigned over the Aegean. His pedigree was impeccable. His father was Zeus, leader of the Gods and his mother was Europa, an exotic Phoenician Princess.

Bulls play a strong theme in this story. Zeus kidnapped Europa disguised as a bull. The transmutation of Gods into animals, and humans merged with animals to become hybrid beasts is also common.

In King Minos' time there was a beast known as a "Minotaur" half man, half bull. He dwelt within an elaborate labyrinth and demanded a tribute (blood sacrifice) from King Minos. This came in the form of several Athenian virgins, male and female. And anyone who entered the Labyrinth soon got lost and were presumed eaten by the rampaging Minotaur.

This went on for several years until a brave young man called Theseus volunteered to be one of the groups of sacrificial youths. When King Minos' daughter Ariadne spies the handsome Theseus, she immediately falls in love. Not wanting her new beau to be devoured by a ferocious monster she decides to aid him. So, she gives him a thread to cast behind so he would not lose his way back out of the labyrinth. Thus equipped, Theseus hunts the Minotaur.

He eventually encounters it, fights then defeats it. Following his thread back, the victorious hero takes Ariadne with him and leaves Crete. But he did not head back to Athens with her and live happily ever after. Instead, he abandons her on a large island in the Cyclades called Naxos, approximately 200 km north of Crete.

This was the official version. Homer embellishes the tale a bit. In the Odyssey, Homer has Ariadne mysteriously put into a deep sleep forcing Theseus to leave Ariadne on a small island called Dia, off the coast of Crete and opposite Amnisos, which was the port of Knossos.

A labyrinthine palatial structure was discovered in the ruins of Knossos, first by Heinrich Schliemann and later, more extensively by Sir Arthur Evans. As a child, Evans read the Homeric tales and continued to believe the site existed and one day he would find it. Its size and grandeur suggested that it was the capital of a vast empire. Evans' would term this the "Minoan civilization". It was estimated as existing from 3000 BCE to around 1100 BCE.

We can clearly see from this account, how myths have influenced an archaeologist's career. Other archaeologists would use the Old Testament as a map for locating major cities like Megiddo and Jericho, in the ancient kingdom of Israel.

If myths have presented archaeologists with a roadmap of sorts, why shouldn't we allow them to guide us? When excavations yield evidence of vast empires, built with a precision unachievable even with today's technology – shouldn't we ask how they did it? When we witness in cave after cave, on innumerable rocks and great plains artwork depicting the visitations of Gods – why shouldn't we take them at their word?

Our ancestors did not just leave us with vague clues here and there. They left us with monuments all over the planet, specifically designed to weather millennia. They may have hoped we would know that greater ages existed in our distant past, triggering us to remember our vast abilities and understanding our greatness.

CREATION STORIES

Creation stories are in every culture, outlining stories of emergence and beginnings, stories of the creator gods. *The Rig Veda* of India, the Egyptian *Atum* and the Hebrew Genesis are examples of creation myths.

Legends and Myths are told repeatedly and in each telling the story shifts slightly from the original. Following are examples of local Native American legends.

YAVAPAI CREATION STORY

PETROGLYPHS, GRAPEVINE CANYON, SPIRIT MOUNTAIN, NEVADA

A Native American creation story tells of Sedona as a place of emergence of the goddess Komwidapokuwia (or Kamalpukwia), which means "first people with medicine" or "old lady rock." Another creation story told by Mike Harrison and John Williams (Yavapai/Apache) states:

> *We came out at Sedona, the middle of the world. This is our home. We*
> *call Sedona "Wipuk." We call it after the rocks and the mountains here.*
> *All Yavapai come from Sedona. But, in time they spread out.*

The Yavapai are native to Sedona and the group of the Yavapai living in Sedona call themselves the Wipuka, highlighting this connection.

According to Yavapai legend, the Lady of the Pearl was sealed in a log with a woodpecker and sent from Montezuma Well to prepare for a Great Flood. For days and nights to follow, it rained incessantly, and the waters of the flood rose covering every landform on Earth. The rain finally stopped after 40 days, and when the water receded the log came to rest in Sedona. A beautiful young maiden was freed from the log by the woodpecker. The Lady of the Pearl was guided by the woodpecker to the summit of Mingus Mountain. Her people had given her a white stone or Pearl for protection and this she carried with her. On Mingus Mountain she met the Sun and they fell in love. She bathed in an enchanted and magical pool in Boynton Canyon when she returned to Sedona. After this, the Lady of the Pearl became pregnant and birthed a daughter who became known as the *First Lady* and mother to all the Yavapai people.

Three sites are mentioned in this creation story: Montezuma Well, Sedona (Boynton Canyon) and Mingus Mountain. Water is also a principle element of the legend siting both the sacred cenote at Montezuma's Well and the sacred spring in Boynton Canyon. The cliff dwellings at Montezuma's Well, in Boynton Canyon, and the hilltop settlement at Tuzigoot may have existed as sacred structures. Pilgrims seeking inspiration, healing, guidance, or wisdom may have lodged at these dwellings for a time, just as today's visitors to Sedona and the Verde Valley find lodging to undertake their spiritual journey in the area.

HOPI CREATION STORY

Tawa, the Sun God and Spider Woman (Kokyanwuhti), the Earth Goddess were alone in the beginning. Tawa controlled the powers and mysteries in the world above—Spider Woman controlled the magic of the world below. In this time there was no other living thing—neither man nor woman, bird nor beast. Only the two that existed could will all else into being.

One day they decided there should be other gods to share their labors. Tawa divided himself and Muiyinwuh, God of All Life Germs emerged. Spider woman divided herself and Huzruiwuhti emerged as a Woman of Hard Substances (turquoise, coral, shell, silver, etc.) Tawa made Huzruiwuhti his wife and they birthed Puukonhoya, the Youth and Palunhoya, the Echo, and later, Hicanavaiya, Man-Eagle, Plumed Serpent, and many others.

Spider Woman and Tawa sat and thought together and decided they would make the earth to be between the Above and Below. Spider Woman formed the features of the earth from clay and Tawa thought of how things should look. Tawa saw animals, beasts and plants and as his visions grew Spider Woman formed each one from clay. When they were done, they made great magic together and breathed life into the creatures Spider Woman had formed.

Tawa decided they should make creatures in their image to oversee all the rest. Spider Woman formed them from clay and again the two breathed life into their creations. All the people they created followed Spider Woman as she led them through the four great caverns of the Underworld until they finally came to an opening, a sipapu, which lead to the earth above.

7

PREPARATION FOR ACCESSING SACRED PLACES: SEEN

UXMAL, MEXICO

SPIRITUAL ENERGY EXPANSION NUCLEUS: SEEN

RIVER, VIET NAM

SEEN is a three-step method preparing us to connect with the information and beings at Sacred Places in the invisible realms of existence. The invisible can be seen and so can we. The SEEN method will appear in exercises throughout the book and can be used for any type of divination. The SEEN method fosters a strong and stable energy system for an Integrative Achaeologist.

STEP 1: GROUND

When we ground ourselves, we bring all our aspects into the present time—Now—and we stabilize the physical body. Any excess energy accumulated during sessions or interactions with other beings or dimensions will naturally flow into the earth. Eliminate all distractions and noises, turn off all devices. Enter into silence and close your eyes.

- Keep the spine erect so energy can flow freely.
- If sitting or standing plant the feet firmly on the ground.
- If lying, place the hands and arms at your sides.
- Exhale completely. All the old, tired energy leaves the body and makes way for the new.
- Inhale will happen automatically, filling your chest to abdomen area with new, fresh breath.
- Feel the revitalizing energy entering the body with each breath.
- Invite all beneficial aspects of your multidimensional self to be fully present with you.
- Use a series of eight breaths to feel grounded and centered. Do eight more breaths as needed.
- See a golden cord of light extend from the base of your spine to the center of the earth and up through the top of the head to infinite domain. (This cord can be dematerialized after your session or interaction is complete.)
- Scan the body for any areas of tension, stress, pain, holding or tightness.
- Breathe into any areas of discomfort and as you exhale, release the energy down to the center of the earth where it can be used as fuel or nutrients.
- Enjoy feeling grounded and present.

STEP 2: EXPAND THE ENERGY FIELD

A field of energy surrounds the physical body and contracts and expands with feelings, situations, health, environment, and relationships. We can consciously expand the energy field, making it as large as we desire. When our field is larger, we feel alive, present, centered, and confident—we can vibrate our light and essence more fully.

- After grounding, continue to exhale fully and allow the breath to automatically fill your body.
- With each inhale, imagine the energy field surrounding your body getting larger while simultaneously being filled with light.
- Choose the colors of the rainbow or any single color to fill the field with light.
- Feel the light surrounding you and warming you.
- Expand the energy field a minimum of six feet from your body.
- Circulate the light and energy in your field.
- Flow and move the light within the energy field to continually refresh and restore the physical and mental body while boosting psychic abilities.
- Imagine a waterfall effect where the color of light you have chosen flows downward, upward, or in a circular direction around the body. This vibrant flowing energy field automatically releases anything you no longer need to hold or carry and repels any type of negativity or infringement.
- Relax into the feeling of presence and energy expansion.

STEP 3: HEART-OPENING BREATH

One way to shift to inner knowing is to move our consciousness from the head to the heart—operate from a feeling center rather than left-brain logic. A heart centered reality naturally aligns with the universe and planet. Heart centered awareness illuminates the core and nature of people, places, and events. You will recognize what harmonizes with you and what does not.

The Heart-Opening Breath is a centering, grounding and meditative breath as useful in everyday life as it is on journeys to Sacred Places. The breath clears the mind of chatter, psychological assessment and other distractions and opens the heart. Use this breath any time throughout the day when you want to relax, refocus or come back to center.

- Lying, standing, and sitting are all perfect positions for this practice.
- Close your eyes.
- Place both hands over the heart—the center of the chest.
- Breathe naturally for a minute.
- Feel your chest rising and falling as you inhale and exhale.
- Inhale
- Draw your breath in through the top of your head—the crown chakra.
- See this breath as a beam of cleansing and revitalizing light.
- Choose a color for the light.
- Feel the light sweeping all thoughts away, cleansing the mind.
- See and feel any mental clutter transformed into golden stardust.
- Feel the golden stardust cascade from your mind to your heart, nurturing and revitalizing the heart.
- Exhale, breathing out through your heart.
- Focus on your heart as your chest rises and falls with each breath.
- Breathe in through the crown and out through the heart.
- Continue breathing this way focusing on the heart.
- Feel the warmth, peace and calm when consciousness is heart centered.
- Become aware of heightened sensitivity as you relax deeply.
- Remove the hands from the chest once the breath is stabilized.
- As you exhale through the heart, stream the vibration of love out into the world.

SEEN produces a state of relaxation and heightened sensitivity, supporting communication with all beings: animals, plants, rocks, waters and whatever exists in this or other dimensions. It sets up a frequency and vibration allowing us to commune with invisible worlds.

8

ARRIVING AT
SACRED PLACES

NEWGRANGE, IRELAND*

ARRIVING AT SACRED PLACES

PETRA, JORDAN*

To enter the spirit-mode takes courage. You have to dedicate your life to yourself. This is not an egocentric view, more an act of prayer unto yourself. It does not make you more important than the world you live in, you just become the world you live in. Stuart Wilde

Indigenous people acknowledge and interact with invisible worlds and the beings that inhabit them and base their knowledge of the past on their ways of knowing (oral traditions), legends and myths. They believe the places their ancestors occupied are alive, not dead—and the ancestors still inhabit them. Sacred Places await our visit and the sensitivity and respect we embody honors all.

CREATING AN INTENTION FOR YOUR JOURNEY

TEMPLE, KARNAK, EGYPT

You have made the choice to take a journey.

Everything practical has been arranged; your travel plans are intact. Whether your destination is a walk in the woods or an exotic destination halfway across the world -- making that journey will change you.

When we take a journey we literally, albeit temporarily, pull up stakes and make a geographic move. All that we are connected with and grounded to, shifts. We may cross time-zones, ley-lines and even timelines. We traverse oceans, mountains, continents, and skies.

Whatever the distance or the terrain that new territory will forever be a part of our inner geography. And that new land is alive with healing, wisdom and all sorts of data which has the ability to shift our perspective and priorities.

A journey to a Sacred Place is a big undertaking that involves the rewiring of our internal and interdimensional circuitry. Here, we have a great opportunity to affect seismic personal change and call in upgrades to our lives.

We can receive an optimum return by creating an intention or a set of intentions for our journey. Here are some examples:

- What would you like to see, know, or understand on this journey?
- What would you like to call into your life now?
- Are there specific changes that you would like to experience in yourself?
- Do you need help or assistance of some kind?

Be creative in your questing. There are no limits to what you might imagine or desire to receive from such a journey. Take the time to write it out before you leave home. Have clarity about what you desire and keep your intention present with you like a prayer.

In this way, your higher self, guides, allies, ancestors – whomever, whatever, can be apprised of what you intend and be of assistance in helping to bring that forward in your life.

CREATING A PROTECTIVE SHIELD

Shields are created to protect you from any interference, negativity or unwanted energy that may be present. When you step into multidimensional reality you encounter beings of all kinds and some may carry energy that is not beneficial or supportive. Psychics often create a shield when entering these realms, as do shamans. Here are two easy ways to create a shield that will protect you on any ventures into other realms:

Use the Heart Opening Breath to relax and become present.

Imagine your energy field as it surrounds you and with each successive exhale, expand your energy field to the exact size that feels right for you.

MIRRORS: Create a net-like weaving around the outer edges of your energy field – use golden threads and tiny mirrors of any size and shape you find pleasing. The tiny mirrors work to defect any unwanted beings or energies that may attempt to intrude into your space—consciously or unconsciously. The shining mirrors are not only beautiful—they protect you.

ROSES: Visualize a perfect rose. The rose holds the highest vibration of the flower kingdom and the red rose is often used to symbolize the mystic center. Create a net-like weaving of red roses to surround your expanded energy field. A rose shield will confine your spiritual essence, adding strength and courage and keep any unwanted intrusions away.

This process will only take a couple minutes. When you have completed your work or research, you can de-materialize the shield. Use a shield any time you find yourself in an environment or around people whose energy, words or actions are less than uplifting and positive.

CLEANSING YOUR ENERGY FIELD

Should you pick up any unwanted energy a salt bath is always an easy and effective way to cleanse the field. Smudging (burning incense or plant materials) and passing the smoke through your energy field is another ay to remove any unwanted energy. Spraying a flower essence into the field also works and many fine products are available—or make your own. We pick up energy from others and situations throughout our day, so it is a good practice to cleanse our energy field daily.

HONORING THE GUARDIANS

All Sacred Places have guardians who oversee and monitor comings and goings. There are actual human guardians and those that are invisible to us. Even if you do not believe such things, it is customary and wise to honor the guardians before entering a Sacred Place.

AUSANGATE, SACRED MOUNTAIN, PERU*

Peru 2009

A few years ago, I met a man in South America who told me a story. Juan had no spiritual leanings and beliefs about the invisible worlds. However, he lived his entire life in Cuzco, Peru, with a view of Ausangate, the sacred mountain, and he knew he would visit it one day.

Years later, he bought a new truck and felt confident about making a journey to the mountain. He set off and, try as he might, he lost his way several times and found himself driving away from the mountain rather than toward it. Juan was determined to reach the mountain and minutes after he turned on to a different road, the axle on the truck broke. He had to call for help and abandon the journey

Some months later, still enthusiastic about visiting the mountain, Juan, through the advice of a friend, enlisted the services of a local shaman. The shaman had an old car that could barely make it on paved roads and Juan immediately began to doubt his choice. Together, they struck out on roads that appeared impassible. From time to time, the shaman would stop the car and get out. He said prayers and made coca leaf offerings to rocks or trees in unmarked paces alongside the road. These, Juan was told, were guardians of the sacred mountain.

The shaman was able to maneuver the old car over the rough terrain and eventually situated it and the passengers within 600 feet of the base of the mountain—much closer than Juan ever imagined possible.

Juan looked at me while he was telling the story and said, "I did not believe in these things, invisible guardians and spirits of a place. After making this journey with the shaman to the sacred mountain, I know they do exist and if they are not honored, access may not be possible."

In our excitement to enter the site, we do not want to overlook this primary step. Take a few moments to acknowledge the guardians, ask for passage and protection and express gratitude. Here is an example of a simple greeting to extend before entering:

- Guardians of the ancient cities and sacred lands, especially, (name the site).
- My name is:
- I ask your permission, protection, and blessing to enter here today.
- State your intention for the visit (for example: prayer and thanksgiving, renewal, remembrance, insight, wisdom, inspiration, healing, exploring, clarity).
- I ask that you guide me to the location(s) at the site that will help me to achieve my purpose and assist me to fully receive the benefits of this visit.
- I thank you for preserving the energetics of the site and allowing me to enter. I am grateful for your presence here.

ENTERING SACRED PLACES

The energy fields of Sacred Places are finely tuned to recognize and receive visitors who have been appearing for hundreds or thousands of years. While the crowds may storm through the gateway the minute it opens as they would on a sale day at a department store, an attitude of reverence is one of the gifts you can bring to Sacred Places. Basic guidelines follow:

*Be it temple, pyramid, mountain, or stream, we meet our ancestors, guides, allies,
god, goddess, higher power, and the Eternal Divine Self when we visit.*

Pause in the general area of the site or at the entryway. When visiting an old friend, we would not barge through the door without announcing ourselves. The same is true at Sacred Places.

OFFERINGS

Offerings can be presented to the guardians before entering and again at any location within the grounds.

Determine, in advance, what offering might be traditional or customary and comply with the custom or tradition. Buddhist temples in Asia sell incense to visitors to burn in a large receptacle before entering. Candles are sold outside churches and cathedrals.

Visitors place them in a holder that is provided inside the building and pray. Coca leaves are used in Peru in specific ways by Curanderos. Tobacco and cornmeal are used by Native Americans. These biodegradable and earth-based offerings are used in a tiny amount (for example—a pinch of cornmeal) and placed in an inconspicuous place.

Unless instructed as to the proper use and placement of offerings, do not leave visible offerings at the sites. If you have a biodegradable offering, prepare it as follows.

- Place the offering in the hands and place the hands over the heart.
- Use the Heart-Opening Breath to transfer your love and essence into the offering.
- Extend the offering to the earth or guardians.
- Do not leave anything visible at the site or bury objects. Foreign objects, including crystals and stones left at the sites, interfere with the frequency and intention of the Sacred Place.

BALINESE FULL MOON OFFERINGS BEING CARRIED TO THE CEREMONIAL SITE*

LEAVE IT WHERE YOU FIND IT

Dirt, rock, stones, or artifacts—whatever exists at a location is to remain at that location. Upon the return of several crystals to the Kogi in Columbia, they were able to facilitate four rivers to spring from the earth. The stones, and artifacts, according to the Kogi, are part of the place they came from. Taking anything away from an area, including many objects that now rest in museums, compromises the well-being of an area.

FINDING YOUR PLACE(S)

- Hold an intention to make a clear and strong connection with the site and to be led to the perfect location for your purpose.
- Walk slowly, feeling each footstep connect with the earth.
- Stop, sit or stand periodically as guided to do so.
- Wander through the site, feeling the way rather than following along or rushing. Stop to meditate or to gaze over the site.
- Sense and feel the perfect place to be in: a cave to sit in, a place to lie down on the earth, sitting or standing beside a wall.
- There is no right way to do this—trust your Inner Knowing.

An individual place of power at a Sacred Place may not be anywhere near the main site, temples, shrines, or ceremonial areas.

Dowse to locate your perfect place and take the time needed to explore and sense.

CEREMONIES

Sacred Places have been the repositories of ceremonies for millennia. A ceremony can be anything from a simple, silent prayer to a complex and elaborate production. When we visit Sacred Places, we step into the aura or field of many ceremonies of the past. What do we want to add to this if anything?

Words or prayers of acknowledgment, truth, and gratitude spoken
from the heart are always an appropriate ceremony.

Respect for indigenous people, their land, rituals and ceremonies, is essential. Overlaying ceremonies of our own is not recommended or welcomed at many Sacred Places. An experienced local ceremonialist, shaman or medicine person will know how to address the site, call forth the guardians and energies, make the appropriate offerings and assist you to receive value from the experience.

9

THE SACRED EARTH

KIVAS, CHACO CANYON, NEW MEXICO

ACCESSING THE SACRED EARTH

KIVA, CHACO CANYON, NEW MEXICO

Mystery, legends, and the lure of Sacred Places draw us to them. From the comfort of our home, we travel great distances to see and feel what the pictures and stories cannot tell us—to discover our own special relationship to these mystical places. Integrative Archaeologists want to do more than simply "see" a site and take a photograph to remember they did so.

Focusing your intention and allowing adequate time will be most important. You may not have a specific intention in mind other than to receive what the sites, ancestors and guardians must tell or show you. To access this information, you may need time to lie down, meditate, write or telepath with the elements of the structures at places you choose to visit.

You may have travelled a great distance to connect with a Sacred Place and receive its messages or healing. Be gentle with yourself and follow your intuition and heart. Take the time you need to receive what you came for.

Suggestions follow for accessing Sacred Places. You will find your own way and develop your own methods as you continue to visit and work with sites. As you use the methods in this book, you will discover where your strengths and interests lie. Have fun on your exploration and dig deeper into the past. Find ways to use and share the information you can detect. Methods in this chapter can be applied at any type of Sacred Place anywhere in the world. Take this book with you and use it as you travel.

ARTIFACTS

In Vancouver, B.C. looking at the Inuit objects in the museum, I stopped several times. At the sight of a certain mask, I could hear singing and chanting—a beautifully carved paddle pulled me to a shoreline where I saw its carver working to reveal its perfection. Alongside, were the tools being used and a couple bowls of pigment to be used to highlight the imagery.

Looking further I could see this paddle was being made to be used at an upcoming ceremony. The images revealed a bird and the heart of the carver showed me this amazing paddle was to lift the spirit of the bird higher and to lift the heart of the owner higher as well.

An artifact is an object made by a human being, typically one of cultural or historical interest. Artifacts can be ritual or ceremonial objects, weapons, decorations, jewelry, masks, weavings, paintings, statues, pottery, or other items reflective of the past. Traditional archaeologists recover artifacts and use them to piece together the history and customs of a place or culture. Like puzzle pieces, these fragments fit together to reveal a story.

Is there a museum attached to or nearby the place you will visit? Spend some time with the artifacts on display as they may become an important part of your research. Whether your quest is personal, or you are seeking information of lost civilizations and hidden histories, the resources at museums can be of great value. Although, in many situations, the artifacts are encased or protected in some way, you can still create a connection. If you are visiting a place where artifacts are available to be touched—great!

Integrative Archaeologists find the contents of museums endlessly informative and inspiring. A visit to a museum before or after visiting a site will add dimension to your experience. Many of the artifacts preserved in these locations are "alive" and broadcasting information. Locating those artifacts that may have resonance or meaning for you is a matter of attraction.

Artifacts are amazing sources of information and enlightenment. If you draw, you might like to make a drawing of those that are most powerful for you. Photographs can be taken in some museums and these can be helpful in your studies.

The field of traditional archaeology presents us with these pieces of the past and we are extremely fortunate to be able to see them. They help to trigger memories and provide us with information on many more levels than the descriptions they bear. You may find objects you know you were connected with, objects that were yours in some other life.

What calls to you as you walk through the display? There may be dozens of objects in one case, so take the time to allow your eyes and consciousness to take in each one individually. Often, an object will draw you right in.

ARTIFACTS, LIMA MUSEUM

HOW TO CONNECT WITH ARTIFACTS

Here are suggestions to use when visiting a museum or other site where artifacts are on display.

- Allocate plenty of time for your exploration of artifacts.
- Initiate SEEN and continue using the Heart-Opening Breath.
- Walk slowly and read the descriptions of artifacts that attract you.
- Descriptions may include an age, use, purpose, material, location, or other information.
- Close your eyes and connect with the object while continuing the Heart-Opening Breath.
- Notice in your mind's eye how the object appears to you. It may become animated, show you colors it once wore, its owner, its use.
- Speak to the object, telepathically asking any question you might have, for example:
- What was your original use or purpose?
- Do you still hold the power you were imbued with?
- Do you have a story to tell or wisdom to impart to me?
- Can I connect with you to share healing?
- What else can you tell me?
- Do you know of civilizations much older than the time you were created?
- What places are best for me to visit at the site you are from?

Your own set of questions will develop based on your interests and what you are seeking at the time. Allow the telepathic conversation to flow.

SACRED MOUNTAINS

Our Sacred Spirit put us on these Six Sacred Mountains (the sacred mountains of the Four Corners Area of the American Southwest). And the Six Sacred Mountains are not outside us—they are inside. Katherine Smith Yinishye, Big Mountain Navajo

Spiritual explorers are naturally drawn to reaching the heights. Climbing mountains helps to transcend this earthly existence—if just for a little while.

Mountains and mountaintops stretch from the earth and reach toward the stars—a desirable location for the ancients and a destination for life after death. Taller than the surrounding landmass, a mountain top has always been considered a place closer to Source. To reach this pinnacle is, at once, a challenge, a relief and, finally—a victory. The air is purer, cleaner, and thinner vision is enhanced. Surely, being at such heights is being in the place of the gods.

Mountaintops are closer to the sun, our definitive and ever-present source of power and light. Civilizations around the world have worshiped the sun as god, and great temples and pyramids were built to honor this life-giving golden light representing the creator.

Mountains are places of deep connection with the Self and Source. We climb a mountain to gain a more finely tuned perspective, achieve greater clarity and initiate healing or change. On a mountaintop our ability to meditate is enhanced and we experience elevated thoughts.

MACHU PICCHU, AGUAS CALIENTES, PERU

According to Taoist belief, mountains are a medium of communication between people, the immortals, and the primeval powers of the earth.

Practitioners of Feng Shui (also known as Geomancy) consider mountains to be powerful sites of telluric power, a sacred force of energy running through the earth itself. This energy is also known as dragon energy. According to these practitioners, the dragon current is of two kinds, yin (feminine) and yang (masculine), and mountains are regarded as embodying the yang.

Spending time at the heights lifts the spirit and broadens perspective. If you have a mountain visit on your agenda, plan to spend time once you reach the summit.

Lie down on the earth and connect with the strength and wisdom of the mountain. Meditate, pray, or do whatever you feel will connect you more deeply. Know that you can leave the past behind and walk into a new beginning as you make your way down the mountain.

MOUNTAIN CLIMBING SAFETY

Mountains present us with more of a physical challenge than simply walking through a site. Mountain paths can be rugged with many loose stones and tiny rocks. Be well prepared for your climb. Become aware of the climate and the changes in temperature throughout the day. Here are some suggestions for the mountain climbing enthusiast:

- Bring layers of clothing—a lightweight fleece and rain jacket that rolls up for easy transport can be lifesavers.
- Drinking water is essential—much water. Dehydration happens quickly and is extremely dangerous.
- Wear shoes with deep cut treads. Flat-bottomed shoes offer no protection or support on the rocky trails and no traction to prevent rolling and slipping.
- A pair of hiking sticks are excellent to bring along.
- Bring your cell phone in case you need to call for help. Find out if there is cell phone service in the area you are addressing.
- Let someone know where you are going and when you expect to be back. This can be a friend or someone at the hotel where you are staying. People get lost and cell phone service is not always available.
- Pack along snacks like protein bars, fruit, and nuts.
- Bring sunscreen and/or a hat. The sun is stronger as you climb higher.
- Bring a small pocket mirror—in the event you are lost or hurt with no cell phone service, signaling aircraft with a mirror can bring help.
- Pack a small flashlight in your bag.
- Avoid climbing on delicate sandstone and limestone structures, spires and buttes—they break apart and crumble easily causing erosion and extreme danger for the climber or hiker.
- Contact the local forest or park service to learn of trail conditions, closures or other current information that will be valuable to your climb.
- Acquire a map of the trail(s).
- Read the section of this book on Outdoor and Site Etiquette. This will clearly outline what you need to know about being outdoors.
- Bring your notebook (paper or electronic) or recording device.

APPROACHING SACRED MOUNTAINS

The journey up a mountain provides an ideal opportunity for the practice of Integrative Archaeology. Ascending the mountain is a time for letting go of anything and everything you no longer need to hold or carry—beliefs, ideas, conditioning, relationships or whatever you are now ready to release. Feel the cleansing in your body, mind and spirit as you release the old and make way for the new.

Each conscious footstep is a prayer. Walk slowly—with the left foot (heel to toe placement) draw the nutrients and healing from the earth. With the right foot release the essence of old, tired energy into the earth. The earth gratefully accepts this gift of energy and converts it to fuel and nutrients.

With each inhale, imagine bringing a sparkling golden light into all aspects of the Self, revitalizing, restoring, and healing from the inside out.

Once at your destination on the mountaintop or somewhere else along the way where you feel drawn to stop, prepare a comfortable place for yourself where you will be undisturbed.

- Initiate SEEN.
- Read the section of this book on Writing with Spirit if your choice is to communicate with the mountain.
- Meditate, pray, use your Divining Skills to access information and receive any messages from the mountain.
- See the section of this book on Interspecies Communication to dialogue with mountains.
- Keep a record of your experience, questions, and answers.

Descend from the mountain slowly and carefully. This is a time of integration, bringing in the new and receiving an expanded vision or reality. As you walk down the mountain, visualize, and feel yourself with the desired changes and upgrades in place.

The journey up and down the mountain allows for an expansion and healing of the Self. Use it wisely; it is good medicine.

ARCHAEOLOGICAL SITES

Precious and fragile archaeological sites exist around the world and millions of visitors are eager to see and experience them. Although archaeological sites are often referred to as ruins, Native Americans and other indigenous people around the world consider these places to be alive and inhabited by their ancestors. Approach and visit these sites with the respect you would accord to an elder or wisdom keeper. Step lightly, listen carefully and express gratitude.

Having the opportunity to stand in the presence of the remains of the distant past is a great gift. Sensitively, we can feel and hear the echoes of ancient civilizations. Our visits to archaeological sites are of great value to us and to the sites.

PUMA PUNKU, TIAHUANACO, BOLIVIA

GUIDELINES FOR VISITING ARCHAEOLOGICAL SITES

Due to vandalism, graffiti, and other destructive acts, we have increasingly more limits placed on our fragile archaeological sites around the world. Visitors are asked to maintain a consciousness of stewardship when visiting these sites. Here is a list of guidelines for visiting an archaeological site:

- Every part of the site is extremely fragile—walls, structures, and the areas around them.
- Climbing, sitting, standing, or leaning on the structures can cause irreparable damage.
- Information is altered forever when we remove artifacts or rocks from the sites. It is not only the archaeological reference that is compromised, but the site and land lose part of their vibration and spiritual integrity.

You may come across petroglyphs and pictographs in the areas you visit; some are thousands of years old. These outdoor museums reflect stories of the past and should be viewed and felt rather than tampered with. Any type of marks, writing, painting, touching, altering, or engaging with these ancient writings creates irreparable damage. Generations to come are denied their experience due to unconscious acts by visitors. Archaeologists lose valuable information. There is no upside to this behavior.

- Take a photo of yourself standing in front of a site if you need to have a reminder that you were there. Writing one's initials on a rock wall, wood-post, historical building, tree, or any monument is egoistical, inconsiderate, and downright stupid.
- During your travels, you may spot artifacts and be inclined to move them or stack them together in another area. There is a story being told in the location of the artifacts and once they are moved, a piece of the past is destroyed forever.
- Digging, dislodging, removing, and piling up of artifacts changes what we might learn about a location. Leave it where it lies.
- Reconstruction of previous environments depends on cultural deposits, including the soil on or at an archaeological site.
- Past environments can be reconstructed by scientifically testing the soil to reveal information (i.e. the types of plants that were used by past inhabitants).
- Carry out any trash (especially organic remains) you may have while visiting a site. Always bring an extra plastic bag to carry out trash others may have left. This is a great help in discouraging the practice of littering.
- Stay on designated trails. There are fragile desert plants and soils that are part of archaeological sites and they are destroyed when you stray from the trail. Trails are there for your protection.
- Small desert birds and snakes make their homes under rocks, in burrows and bushes. These environments are precious to the animals and we want to take care not to disrupt or destroy their homes and lives.
- Fire destroys prehistoric organic materials, ruins the dating potential of artifacts and damages, or even destroys rock art and the history left for all to enjoy and discover. Absolutely no fires, candles, or smoking should occur at archaeological sites.
- Meanings of images and symbols painted and pecked on stones are still being studied. Refrain from touching any rock art as the oils from even the cleanest of hands can cause the images to deteriorate.
- Drawing, painting, scratching, carving, and graffiti destroys rock art and obliterates the messages left to be deciphered.
- Wooden and stone buildings have their stories to tell as well. Refrain from any type of marking or carving on these structures.
- Please leave your pets at home. In their normal routine of digging, urinating, and defecating they can destroy fragile cultural deposits and frighten other visitors and native animals.
- Do not ride or drive your bicycle through archaeological sites.
- Do not camp in a site or dismantle historic buildings for firewood or any other use.

APPROACHING ARCHAEOLOGICAL SITES

Archaeological sites require us to be super sensitive. They are delicate environments and receive much human traffic due to tourism. Silence is a great practice when visiting archaeological sites—let the stones speak to you.

Interacting with archaeological sites is a rare opportunity to sense the past. The earth and the stones await—steeped in multidimensional memories and information. It is not necessary to touch the stones directly to commune with them.

- See book section: Entering Sacred Places.
- Initiate SEEN.
- Open the hands, palms facing toward the rock or structure. Vibrations, messages, and images can be received while holding the palms of the hands six inches or more away from the rock or structure.
- Close the eyes and concentrate on the center of the palms of the hands as being an active receptor of information coming from the rocks or structures. You may feel warmth or a slight vibration in the palms of the hands. Allow the connection between your hands and the structure to develop.
- With your eyes closed, look up toward the center of the forehead.
- Notice if there are any colors, words, visions, or messages appearing. This could take a few minutes, so take your time and be patient.
- Simultaneously, notice any signals from the body, areas of discomfort or tightness. Tune into body signals and see if there is a message there, a memory, a vision.
- Remain sensitive.
- Telepathy and other Divining Skills can be employed to connect with archaeological sites, specific stones, doorways, altars, ceremonial sites, images, or artifacts.
- If a location exists where you will be undisturbed, practice meditating and dreaming.
- Afterwards, if feasible, sit or lie on the earth. Connecting the body with the earth is always desirable. Position yourself out of the flow of traffic and away from the structures. Nearby is close enough.
- See the section of this book on Interspecies Communication to dialogue with the archaeological site.
- Use the Writing with Spirit exercise to dialog with the site, makers of the images, guardians, ancestors, or previous residents.
- Record your experience.
- Leave a prayer of gratitude and blessing.

SACRED WATERS

Water immediately connects us to all life, to Source.

All water is sacred. Sacred bodies of water present themselves in all sizes and shapes, covering an estimated 75 percent of the planet. Springs, rivers, lakes and streams crisscross our world, weaving intricate patterns above and below the earth's surface. In all cultures, the miraculous emergence of living water is seen as the matrix of life itself and the qualities of purification, healing and regeneration naturally follow. Water is alive, intelligent, evolving and nourishes all life. We can plant a seed, but without the addition of water, it is unlikely to grow. We are seeds of the earth also, and with water we are nurtured, sustained, supported, and thriving.

Water holds a mystery in its depths. It can be soft and embracing if entered gently and hard as a rock when we smash into it. Raging waters can destroy buildings, property, and lives in an instant. Healing waters have curative powers that transcend what modern medicine has to offer. What a delicious mystery this water is.

Water, within its liquid crystalline essence, holds the thriving vibrations and patterns of every plant, animal, mineral and human that has ever lived upon the earth.

Apart from the life-giving qualities of water, healing and divination are traditional virtues of water. Explorers of all descriptions visit the waters, drink of it, bathe in it or take to it in times of stress or when healing or clarity is needed or desired.

Ancient and contemporary indigenous cultures consider water sacred and curative and treat it with great reverence.

Ceremonies and gatherings have been taking place for tens of thousands of years at water sites. Sacred Places are often located above an underground stream or the confluence of two underground bodies of water. Our connection to water may involve immersing ourselves in its pure liquid crystalline essence, having a drink, sprinkling a few drops into our energy field or walking along the shoreline.

APPROACHING SACRED WATERS

Water is a powerful carrier of information, a source of inspiration and healing. Here are suggestions for interactions with water:

- Refer to the Entering Sacred Places section of this book.
- Bring warm clothing or a blanket.
- Find a quiet spot, sit, or lie down.
- Initiate SEEN.
- See and feel the flowing water washing away all that is no longer necessary to hold in your body, mind, or life.
- Feel the fresh flowing water bringing in new energy and wellbeing, restoring and revitalizing every part of the body, mind, and spirit.
- Open to what your meditation provides.

- Refer to the Interspecies Communication section of this book to dialogue with the water.
- Refer to Writing with Spirit to initiate a dialogue with water.
- Dreaming near water is an excellent way to receive our next steps or gain insight into areas of our lives or relationships.
- Find a place where you can lie down and be comfortable and undisturbed for some time.
- Look at the section of this book on Dreaming for complete instructions.

Bathing in the waters can be a time of meditation, whether you are simply soaking your feet or immersing your full body. Healing energy is strong at water sites. Speak to the spirits of water; ask for their assistance in healing on physical, emotional, or other matters.

RIVER TEMPLE, VIET NAM

SACRED STONES

Stones are enduring libraries holding the ancient wisdom of extreme human antiquity. Walk among the stones, connect with them, listen to their stories.

Stones have been venerated since the earliest times. Worship of stones is found in most ancient cultures and mentions of stones are found in most of the world's religions. Stones and crystals are liquefied minerals that have hardened in the earth's atmosphere. As self-contained energy systems, they make excellent conductors for electro-magnetic waves and currents.

Indigenous cultures see stones as living beings, wisdom keepers.

Stones of all sizes and shapes make up the mystical landscape of Sacred Places. Whether you are looking at natural structures or the massive remains of lost civilizations–from the mightiest to the tiniest, each stone carries a vibration and has a story to tell.

Sonic signatures on gems and minerals can be read and interpreted.

The ancients often marked with stones those places on the earth emanating powerful frequencies. Monuments of stone and circles of stone are found throughout the world marking Sacred Places for successive worshipers and religions for thousands of years.

Romance and mystery attract us to stones. Legends and myths speak of them, their powers, and ceremonial uses. There are also many beliefs and ideas about the power of crystals. Indigenous and aboriginal people have knowledge and remembrance of their existence and use in distant pasts.

The entire world of precious and semiprecious stones is another category of delight. The elaborate crowns worn by monarchs were not purely decorative. The gemstones embedded in the gold, silver or other precious metals were devices to give the monarch a clearer line of communication with Source. The spectacular jewel-studded crowns worn by monarchs, often viewed as part of the regalia, pomp and circumstance are high-powered antennas reaching far into other dimensions.

APPROACHING SACRED STONES

SAQSAYWAMAN, CUZCO, PERU

Apart from the exceptionally large stones in the landscape, there are stones of all sizes offering an opportunity for connection. Pick up a stone and hold it in your hand or place it over the heart or forehead. Breathe and tune into the stone—see what it might have to share. Below is an outline of a process that can be used for stones of any size.

Choose a rock structure or stone you find appealing. It is not necessary to be right next to the stone. You can speak to different stones from one vantage point.

- Initiate SEEN.
- See Interspecies Communication to begin a dialogue with the stones.
- Bring your attention to the inside of your head.
- Look upward between the eyebrows and slightly above.
- Open the crown area at the top of the head and the clairaudient center just above the ears.
- You are now open to receive messages and communication in several ways.
- Refer to the Writing with Spirit section of this book, if that method is of value during this communication.
- Refer to your research questions or use some of these:
- Will you allow me to connect with you?
- Is there anything you would like to tell me about yourself?
- Do you hold wisdom, healing or other energy or information that would be of value to me?

Ask specific questions relating to your circumstances. Certain rocks, like certain people, are more responsive. You may have an opportunity to be closer to a rock or sit near its base. When you feel complete, thank the guardians, the rock itself and leave a prayer of gratitude.

Megalithic stones hold stories
they are libraries of the wisdom of times past
ancients knew the stone would last
when they wrote their stories there

invisible but vibrating
constant multidimensional messaging
some say the Inca built these places
the Inca say
they were built long before

it's in the Earth
the frequency of ancient future wisdom
running down to the core
out to infinite space
a cord that vibrates with each footstep that falls
at sacred places
yours
and mine

stored in precious prisms sparkling beneath the surface
matching transits in the stars and sky
we stand between earth and sky
our Eternal Divine Self
antennae
decoding whispers from other worlds

Luminous Antonio, 2009

EARTH

New ways of perceiving the world and reality are revealed in our earthly walk. Beliefs and expectations play a part in forecasting our experience while the earth connection we make facilitates it.

The earth carries the vibration of ceremonies, dancing, drumming, prayers, hopes and dreams of all who have visited before. The rich and enduring impressions of shamans, medicine people, healers and ceremonialists linger in the canyons, out on the trails and permeate the stones and ancient structures on the earth.

One does not have to go far to tap into the energies of the Earth. Using your intuition and Divining Skills, find a location to explore at a sacred place afar or right near your home.

APPROACHING THE EARTH

If you do nothing else while you visit a Sacred Place, make time for this exercise. You will be greatly rewarded.

- See Entering Sacred Places in the book for information as to how to begin.
- Lying down or sitting on the earth ensures a deep connection.
- Lying face down is ideal, if possible.
- Initiate SEEN.
- Continue the Heart-Opening Breath. Sync your breath and heartbeat with that of the earth.
- Imagine that your body weighs a million pounds and feel it sink more deeply into the earth with each breath.
- Allow self to drift into the vibrant healing energy of the earth.
- See the section of this book on Interspecies Communication to dialogue with the earth.
- Speak to the earth and listen to her stories.

VORTICES

Vortices are high energy spots on the Earth linked by ley lines. A vortex can be visualized as an image of the sun with rays of light emanating from it. Those rays of light are the ley lines, some more powerful than others. In this analogy, the sun is seen as a chakra of the earth and the rays of the sun become the arteries of the body of the earth.

Major vortex areas on Earth are well documented. Vortices exist in all types of terrain—deserts, mountains, volcanoes, hot springs, beneath the ocean, forests, rock outcroppings beneath or near ceremonial sites and temples. Chartres Cathedral in France, some of the Mayan and Egyptian temples and the Potala Palace are examples of Sacred Places built on or near vortex sites.

Next is a list of a few of the major vortex sites in the world.

- Avebury, England
- Ayers Rock, Australia
- Bimini
- Easter Island, Chile
- Machu Picchu, Peru
- Santo Domingo, Dominican Republic
- Sedona, Arizona, USA
- Tibet, Lhasa

As an example of a vortex site, let us look at Sedona, Arizona, USA. "Where's the vortex?" might be the most frequently asked question by visitors to Sedona. Several years ago, a clairvoyant named Paige Bryant studied the energy systems in Sedona and cited certain locations—Bell Rock, Cathedral Rock, Airport Mesa and Boynton Canyon. Visitors consider a trip to one of these places an indispensable part of their journey to Sedona.

VORTEX GATEWAY, SEDONA, ARIZONA

The entire area of Sedona is a vortex, or energy center. The red rocks have an uplifting and clarifying effect on visitors and locals. People feel good just being in Sedona and returning repeatedly to recharge. The refined earth energy has a positive influence on the brain and creates a feeling of wellbeing.

On the planetary grid system map (Becker Hagens, 1983) it is noted that Sedona is one of the five areas in the Northern Hemisphere indicated as a positive healing energy vortex. What does that mean; how does it operate and what will happen when we visit a vortex site? Benjamin Lonetree, scientist and engineer (www.sedonanomalies.com) states:

> "Vortex centers have unique physical properties. Iron-bearing basalt (lava deposits) runs through sandstone, creating magnetic vortices. The red rock spires in the Sedona area are natural formations of this kind. They can be imagined as negatively or positively charged electrodes, carrying current.

> Water, iron, silicon (granite) and traces of copper, silver and gold in the earth create a natural device that attracts and amplifies this electrical energy. The earth discharges this energy, creating a physical or metaphysical occurrence. In other words, the measurable energies rising from the earth in Sedona touch back down into the earth at a location nearby.

> Humans embody oxygen, silicon and iron in their blood, cell salts and glands that rest in the positions of the chakras. The correlations between these materials of the earth and the human body build a harmonic resonance. The vortex energies of Sedona amplify the human psychic centers allowing for a connection between the different dimensions."

Access to these unseen dimensions can come as dreams, visions, heightened awareness, mental clarity, a sense of wellbeing, communications with spirits and beings in other dimensions, instantaneous healing, expanded possibilities, emotional release, stepping out of linear time or other upgrades to the human experience.

APPROACHING VORTICES

Dowsing is an excellent way to locate vortex energy and find a location that is right for you. When visiting a vortex, it is valuable to understand that the earth's energy is not static, it moves. Use your sensitivity or dowse to find a place of power where you will be comfortable to meditate and connect. Choose a time or area with the least amount of people and distractions.

Meditating or connecting deeply at a vortex or energy site opens a portal to tap into higher dimensions. Both humans and the earth have at least 12 layers of subtle bodies along with a current physical body. Being close to an active chakra of the earth (vortex), we can grasp the multidimensional and ever-changing nature of life.

- Lying down or sitting on the earth ensures an excellent connection. Lying face down, connecting through the heart with the earth is ideal, if possible.
- Initiate SEEN.
- Concentrate on the heart area and sync your breath with the heartbeat of the earth.
- Expand your awareness down into the earth and the surrounding surface area.
- Take all the time you need to totally let go, merge fully with the vortex and enjoy.
- Vortices are excellent energy systems to support your meditation including any requests for clarity or healing you might desire to make.

Sacred Places are the repositories for planetary wisdom, just as we are. When you visit or interact with the special energies of such places and their guardians, always leave a prayer of gratitude and blessing behind. Acknowledgment of the exchange that has taken place honors everyone.

10

THE PRACTICE OF INTEGRATIVE ARCHAEOLOGY

TEMPLE OF TRES VENTANAS, MACHU PICCHU, PERU

INTEGRATIVE ARCHAEOLOGY

DELPHI, GREECE*

Integrative Archaeology empowers us to reclaim our innate abilities to connect with the Earth, Sacred Sites and Power Places; ultimately ourselves. It is a personal, multidimensional, multi-sensory search and exploration into the invisible realms of existence to discover our true origins, hidden histories, customs, abilities, practices and deeper meanings beyond the material evidence of ancient and prehistoric civilizations and cultures.

The only degree required to be an Integrative Archaeologist is a desire and willingness to expand our innate sensitivity. We have been desensitized culturally, generationally, educationally and through religions and beliefs. Add to that the many "screens" we interact with; phones, computers, devices. Our ability to connect with and sense the rich universes, unseen worlds and beings that surround us is usually denied and systematically squashed by consensus reality. Yet, many of us have had flashes of insight, dreams, moments or experiences we cannot fit into the "normal" goings on of life. We know there is more.

Integrative Archaeology is an opportunity to fine tune our senses – re-install important parts of our efficient and complex operating system. There is no right or wrong in this quest, because it is a personal one where information and insights gathered are germane to each person's life.

Simply put, we sensitize deeply and learn to trust our inner knowing and perceptions. Instinct, intuition and insight come to the forefront of our perception and allow us to transcend the layers of conditioning that keep us trapped.

Integrative Archaeology enhances our experience of ways Sacred Places can be enjoyed and explored, and can be a perfect vehicle for change and personal growth in our lives.

However, these may only be side effects of a deeper quest to discover hidden histories, ancestors and our unique connections to Sacred Places.

Traditional interpretations do not always recognize the spiritual energies or the wealth of information present in unseen realms at archaeological sites. Integrative Archaeology explorations present us with additional sources of information: remembrances, stories, feelings, and visions that are most relevant to our personal myths and our unique, individual, evolutionary process. "His" story (history) is not Our story and while they are all stories, more value can be derived from our unique personal discoveries.

The old paradigm of being led around like sheep and adapting to
obsolete cultural models and outdated conditioning has ended.

Integrative Archaeologists come from every educational background, religion, belief system, nationality, and age group. They instinctively know that the timeless wisdom traditions of the ancients reflect the highest potential of the human spirit for internal peace, happiness, and the inspired expression of spirit in the material world. Practitioners of Integrative Archaeology know that the past is not behind us, the future is not ahead, and that we are living in the ever-present Eternal Now.

Integrative Archaeologists examine, decipher, translate, and interpret
information based on individual understandings and beliefs. Interpretations
may not match those of others and that is as it should be.

How did our ancestors answer humanity's fundamental questions? Is this all there is? Why am I here, and what is my purpose? Is there something greater in the universe that compels me? What happens after death? Have I been here before? What is the most important thing for me to know right now?

We are destined to find our own answers, live fearlessly in the truth of who we are and take a bit of wisdom from those who came before.

An Integrative Archaeologist may choose to investigate specific people, events or civilizations and access subtleties, thoughts, beliefs, and practices. Individual discoveries might include one's role in the community, relationships, ritualistic practices and more. Cosmic principles and learning can be acquired, leading to well-being. It is not unusual to receive information that contradicts the mainstream viewpoints of historians and traditional archaeologists.

INTEGRATIVE ARCHAEOLOGY PRINCIPLES

One's destination is never a place, but a new way of seeing things. Henry Miller

As Integrative Archaeologists, we model new behaviors and ways of visiting and interacting with Sacred Places and the people of the lands on which they rest. Below are the basic principles to follow:

- *Environment:* Learn about environmental sustainability and natural habitats and become familiar with the delicate environments to be visited.
- *Impact:* Integrative Archaeology takes us to natural, fragile, pristine, and protected areas including tribal lands, archaeological sites, and cultural heritage sites. Our visits to these areas are done on a small scale—small numbers of people or larger groups split into smaller groups—to reduce effects on delicate environments.
- *Indigenous Customs:* Honor the local customs, traditions, beliefs, and intentions for the site. Be sensitive and respectful. Honor differences. Indigenous people are often the caretakers and stewards of Sacred Places. If you do not know, ask.
- *Inclusion:* Acquire permission to enter specific areas or locations. Welcome the participation of the local people and invite them to lecture, speak or guide. Invite local shamans, medicine people and elders to perform ceremonies and share stories and traditions.
- *Respect:* Do not override or overlay traditions, ceremonies, rituals and customs practiced and maintained by local people.
- *Pay it Forward physical:* We receive wonderful, life changing gifts from the locations and cultures we visit. Find ways to provide direct financial benefits for conservation and/ or to benefit local people or causes in the locations visited.
- *Pay it Forward spiritual:* When we ask for or seek something from Sacred Places, it is customary to return a gift. All interactions with Sacred Places, invisible guardians of sites and any inter-dimensional beings are sacred. Your gift can be a prayer of gratitude and blessing.
- *Representation:* Be impeccable with what you do and say. Our actions inform the behaviors of others.

- *Assumptions:* Assume nothing; always ask. For example, taking photos of tribal or indigenous people is not always an acceptable practice. In some cultures, it is not allowed. In other places, people expect payment for allowing you to take a photo.
- *Site Etiquette:* Read the last section of this book on outdoor and site etiquette.

GENERAL PREPARATION

The goal of life is to make your heartbeat match the beat of the universe, to match your nature with nature. Joseph Campbell

Anticipation is part of the journey—a kind of pre-journey—sparking our enthusiasm and inspiring us. The preparation we make in advance builds excitement and supports us to transition gracefully to our destination. Presented here are options you can choose to exercise. This is not a task list.

BEING INFORMED

If you enjoy research and reading, information gathering will be fun for you. It will bring a rich awareness to the place(s) you plan to visit. Begin researching weeks or months before the actual journey. If you are not inclined to this type of pre-discovery, guiltlessly skip over this section. This is not a requirement—only a suggestion.

A psychological, emotional, and psychic adjustment will be taking place as you allow your imagination prior entry to Sacred Places you plan to visit.

Informing ourselves by exploring the historical, anthropological, archaeological, cultural, and spiritual dimensions of Sacred Places all contribute to our ability to link up with what is available to us personally. Each site holds invaluable treasures and our task is to be the open and willing recipients of those gifts.

Some of the resources available to explore prior findings and perspectives include books, movies, TV, academic journals, magazine articles, online resources, oral histories (audio), previous research and literature. Information derived from this exploration can trigger memories, visions, dreams, or feelings. Embedded in the material are bits of inspiration supporting us to understand our relationship with Sacred Places. This is exactly what we are after. **Categories you may consider pursuing include the following:**

Science—Ethnographic, biological, geological, ecological, geophysical, and paleontological data, among others, can be important to an understanding of the human past.

History—comprises the events, patterns, and processes of the human past, including those that have affected literate societies and those that have affected preliterate or non-literate groups, whose history is sometimes known as prehistory.

HIEROGLYPHICS STAIRCASE, COPAN, HONDURAS*

Archaeology—material remains (artifacts, structures, artworks, etc.) produced purposely or accidentally by human beings.

Material—actual objects retrieved from a historic property as part of a data recovery program, including, but not limited to, artifacts, byproducts of human activity such as flakes of stone, fragments of bone, architectural materials and details, skeletal material, and works of art.

Myth and Legend—stories grounded in truth provide strong reference points for what has transpired. The entire world and cultures within countries are rich in these stories, passed down in art, written and oral word. Unbelievable today, in view of the world we inhabit, beings (half beast and half human), giants, gods that flew through the sky and lived hundreds of years without aging—all existed and flourished. The worlds they created, built, and lived in—what they believed, achieved and knew, continues to be revealed.

Once you have learned all you have an appetite for, put away
your materials. This journey is all about You.

What you see, intuit, find, know, experience, and come to understand about yourself, the site, and your connection to it is the gold to be mined. This alchemical process begins with an intention.

IDENTIFYING PURPOSE AND INTENT

The choice has been made to go on a journey! Everything practical has been arranged and our travel plans are intact. Whether our destination is a walk in the woods or an exotic place across the world, making that journey will change us. When we take a journey we literally, albeit temporarily, pull up stakes and make a geographic move. All that we relate to and ground to shifts. We may cross time zones, ley lines and even timelines. We traverse oceans, mountains, continents and skies.

Any time in our lives can be used as a platform for change, personal growth, healing, clarity, or renewal. When we visit Sacred Places, our purpose may simply be to enjoy and experience a new place—or we may want something specific. Our priorities will organize themselves according to our purpose and intent.

Whatever the distance or terrain, the new territory will forever be a part of our inner geography; downloading new data which can shift our perspective and priorities. A journey to a Sacred Place can initiate the rewiring of our internal and inter-dimensional circuitry. Here we have a great opportunity to affect seismic personal change and call-in upgrades to our lives. Be creative in your questing. There are no limits to what we might imagine or desire to receive from such a journey. Take the time to meditate and write it out before you leave home. Stay present with your intentions like a prayer. In this way, our higher self, guides, allies, ancestors – whomever, whatever, can be apprised of what we intend and be of assistance in helping bring that forward in our lives.

Here are examples of intentions expressed by explorers

- make life changes
- gain clarity on relationship, career and/or health
- receive next steps
- let go
- to heal—physical, emotional, spiritual
- receive life purpose
- connect with ancestors

Knowing what we want to receive from our time at Sacred Places helps to direct the energies to that purpose. Our great powers of healing and transformation will align with the energy of the places visited to produce the desired results.

RECORD YOUR JOURNEY

Choose a recording device that is comfortable and easy for you to manage. Most smartphones come equipped with recording apps. Some of you may prefer a notebook, a camera (video or still) and traditional voice recorders. Graphite or colored pencils are useful if you like to draw.

Visual records remind us of time spent at a location, how it felt to be there and other details we might easily forget. Sometimes photos record things we do not see at the moment we snap the picture.

You may want to record the Integrative Archaeology methods used to acquire information as well as any feelings or physical sensations you experienced at the site. Personally, I am so happy that I made notes about my travels. Here is one:

Antigua, Guatemala is a Spanish Colonial city, charming and luscious in December's 80 degree temperatures. Copan, Honduras, five hours away by car is in a lush jungle near a river and small town.

Unlike Tikal in Guatemala, where one must walk considerable distances to see the structures, the site at Copan is easily accessible down a loamy soft dirt path. At the end of a dirt path, the main plaza reveals the commanding presence of seven elaborately carved Stelea.

Off to the right of the main plaza the hieroglyphic staircase rises just short of 100 feet high and presents the longest surviving Mayan text written in 2000 glyphs in stone. All the incredibly elaborate and stunningly beautiful Mayan Codex were burned by Catholic missionaries believing them to be the devil's work. Three survived--named after the cities where they are kept—Paris, Dresden and Madrid. A disputed fourth Grolier Codex is in Mexico City. The hieroglyphic staircase tracks the history of the rulers of the city and their works and accomplishments.

Walking, I am connecting with the soft, moist earth that vibrates with colors and sounds of the life that took place there hundreds and thousands of years ago. Standing, sitting, lying down on the earth I listen. No matter what the archaeologists and various histories say, I am certain this place is much older—I can feel the heartbeat of the earth. I can see the riot of life shimmering through the stones.

I lay around in various places, taking in the scenes, sights and sounds as they are presented. Feels like home.

Climbing down to a lower level of the site, I speak to a guard and discover I can pay a bribe to enter one of the pyramidal structures. The guard tells me the archaeologists are working there but they are not around today and for some dinero I can quietly slip in. No questions asked.

The guard pulls a huge canvas covering aside and I am led down a dark passageway where the moisture of the earth gives rise to a tornado of recognizable and unrecognizable smells.

We step through a doorway—turn right and follow a narrow passageway. The flashlight the guard holds is the only beacon. He is talking, I am feeling—tuning into what lies beneath.

On our left is an opening in the wall – was it glassed in or just open? I cannot recall. Seven feet away intricate, brightly painted carvings cover a pyramid standing in silent testimony of another, older time. I could almost reach out and touch it.

A heart opening vibe filled the space. Thankfully, the guard was silent for a few moments. Although I always knew and could sense what was beneath the surface – standing so close to a distant past thrilled me. In a second, worlds within reverberated through the earth.

I cannot recall now, but beneath what I could clearly see were other pyramids three or more, not visible but present.

Beneath it all, I thought, was likely the original stone the Maya used to mark the place where the energy was divined to be spectacular. Where did it begin? When was the first indication that this was a special place? When was the first marker or monument brought to this location and what did it look like? Who indicated this was a special place and why did they decide that, how did they know?

It was clear the guard wanted me out. We were trespassing illegally, and he did not want to get caught. There was little time for much more than a glance but in those moments my quest was deepened.

Another area of the site known as Seplucuras, a mile or so distant from the main site, brought a deepening of connection to Copan.

I walked the site and every structure, each with a stone bed built into a small pyramidal platform. One of these drew me back again and again until I finally sat there for some time. Clearly, I had lived here, most certainly in this structure—some distance from but facing the river. Traditional archaeologists say this was the place of the scribes and aristocracy. I began to write a story of my life there, maybe one day I will finish it.

As I read this now, I want to get on a plane and go back. Take a week or more at Copan, bathe in its secrets and listen to its stories, breath its essence. Clues of a magnificent past await the explorer, and each will have a different story or interpretation of what they remember, see and know.

What has been hidden from sight is dwelling deep in the soul memory. Touching in with Sacred Places triggers emanations of awareness. There is always a structure within or beneath the structure we see--touching into the very essence of the earth which drew the builders to the site.

I felt the sweetness of the site from the moment my feet touched the earth—somewhere there is a video of the whole thing, my camera with photos were lost on the journey back to Antiqua. But at least I have this.

What are your time considerations? Will you be traveling alone, with a group, family, friends? Whatever the configuration, be sure you have adequate time for meditation, contemplation, writing–or whatever suits your style of connecting.

WHAT ABOUT THE CLIMATE, WEATHER, TERRAIN?

Acquire a general description of the location you plan to visit including its size and terrain. Knowing the seasonal climate and prevailing weather is important. A rainy season, for instance, can be a muddy experience, often creating mudslides and other conditions prohibitive to travel.

Apps for mapping, Google Earth, and GIS (geographic information systems) devices can be helpful and fun for explorations.

FIELD PROJECT: RESEARCH DESIGN

A Field Project Research Design helps you determine the things you want to gain from the journey. Writing things out will formalize your intentions. Elements might include:

- Indicating specific locations to explore at the site.
- Methods used to acquire information.
- Desired results of the exploration.

Research designs may be modified once on site, as the course of research yields new findings.

QUESTIONS TO ASK YOURSELF

Integrative Archaeologists are well served by approaching the site with a set of research questions in mind. It is up to you to create and answer your own research questions.

Ask questions about one or more locations at a specific site and decide what information you desire the location(s) to yield. Aim to identify locations, time frames, and activities at specific areas of a site. Your questions can focus on acquiring information of a historical, personal, transformational, or healing nature. Additional research questions can be asked during a visit to a location. Examples of questions:

- How was the site first identified?
- What initially drew people to this site?
- When was the site or location first occupied?
- When was the site (or location at the site) last occupied?
- Were different parts of the site occupied simultaneously, or do they represent separate occupational episodes?
- What types of activities occurred at the site?

- How many people were in residence?
- Was there a difference in status between the people associated with the site?
- How were the different structures used?
- Do different areas of the site have different functions?
- Are there areas of the site with strong healing properties?
- Is there a specific location at the site I should focus upon? Where is it?
- What was the main accomplishment or contribution of the people here?
- Are there areas of the site associated with the lives of persons historically significant? Spiritually significant?
- Are there areas of the site where I should focus my research?
- Are there areas of the site associated with my past?
- Where are these areas?
- When was I here?
- What was my life about during that time?
- What parallels can I draw from that former life to this one?

These are examples—add to or take away from the list. Your questions will help orient you to the site, focus your research and provide answers to your specific questions.

EXPLORING ARTIFACTS

Museums and visitor centers are repositories of artifacts collected from Sacred Places. Books and the internet have a wealth of images to imbibe. Take time to study or connect with these items before, during or after your visit to a site. Make notes and record your interpretations of the artifacts as an Integrative Archaeologist. Can you sense the maker of an artifact, their thoughts, ideas, and intentions?

ARTIFACTS FROM PERU

AFTER YOUR VISIT

A vision turns to tiny particles and vanishes completely.

Impressions and insights often happen quickly and may have unusual qualities, imagery, and content. Whenever possible, make a record immediately. Multidimensional experiences can be as elusive as a dream that fades quickly if we do not speak it or write it down. The notes and records you keep will be invaluable.

SHARING AND QUESTIONING

Whether you go alone or with a friend, partner, or group, make time to discuss your findings. If you travel alone, talk to friends and associates about your experience when you return home. Others often have valuable insights that enhance or clarify a vision or understanding. We enrich each other by sharing.

MESSAGES COME SOONER OR LATER

Sacred Places will share their information, wisdom, and healing in different ways to each of us. Release any expectations around how information will come to you.

Visions, messages, emotional clearings, insights, and healing may happen while at the site—or you may notice that life has changed for the better after returning home. It is not always possible to put experience into words.

TOOLS FOR THE INTEGRATIVE ARCHAEOLOGIST

Wakan Tanka, Great Mystery, teach me how to trust my heart, my mind, my intuition, my inner knowing, the senses of my body, the blessings of my spirit. Teach me to trust these things so that I may enter my Sacred Space and love beyond my fear, and thus Walk in balance with the passing of each glorious Sun. - Lakota Prayer

Sacred Places are a living realm of spirit. Consistent acknowledgment of the presence of ancestors and spirits is openly practiced throughout the world in many cultures. Communication with the spirit world, multidimensional reality and Sacred Places is the practice of an Integrated Archaeologist.

Integrative Archaeologists develop finely tuned sensitivities, use multi-sensory resources, focus inward, and communicate with the spirit world.

Traditional archaeology teaches us history through the collection, organization and presentation of culture finds. The archaeologist studies and interprets material objects that remain to understand a culture, their customs, rituals, and beliefs.

Integrative Archaeology honors all information sources and engages inner knowing and divining to explore the invisible aspects of Sacred Places.

INNER KNOWING

A sense of direct contact with the ultimate reality has always been the realm of mystics and sages. Knowing that unity lies at the heart of the universe and seeing the interconnection of all life is at the core of our perceptive abilities.

The analytical left-brain is masterful at throwing objections in our path, blocking our natural intuition. Our conditioning—cultural, religious, educational, etc.— teaches us to listen to outside sources and authorities and rely upon what they must sell or tell. It takes courage to step away from the norms that society has established, regardless of how constricting they are.

Everyone from movie stars to New Age gurus is perceived as knowing something we do not. While each person you meet or observe in life carries messages of wisdom and enlightenment, they can only reflect or teach what you already know.

Our ability to remain unaffected by good or ill fortune is essential
since neither has meaning in multidimensional reality.

Have you ever read a book, watched a movie, or sat in a workshop only to think I knew that! When tuning into your bodily felt sense of a person or situation, you might have thought: It feels right to me. Developing trust happens over time. You may recognize how many times you knew the truth of a situation and ignored it.

We know who is on the phone before it rings, we think about an old friend and a letter arrives in the mail, the smell of a deceased grandfather's cigar wafts into the room when there is no one nearby.

Teachers and guides are there to remind us of who we are and to open us to new ways of thinking and being. Placing anyone in a position of authority, relying upon answers they provide or being star struck in their presence is a distraction.

You are the only expert on your life, and your inner wisdom
and truth are the gold you are destined to mine.

Higher self, the God presence within, the small still voice, a gut feeling, or hunch is our own inner knowing. Intuition, insight, and instinct are all part of inner knowing. We are not taught or encouraged to honor our inner knowing, but to look for hard evidence and logic from others.

Looking inward for answers and wisdom enables us to enter the realm of our Eternal Divine Self and access unlimited power and wisdom. We can make a conscious upgrade in our operating system whenever we choose. Flip the switch.

We are told things must be seen to be believed rather than
(the truth) things have to be believed to be seen.

MIND THE MIND

If you correct the mind, the rest will fall into place. Lao Tzu

Become consciously aware of where your thoughts are focused. Listening to, watching, or being engaged with disempowered static frequencies of fear, issues, dramas, problems, challenges and inner critic or confusion blocks the stream of life supporting information that is trying to make its way to you. We are free when we become the neutral observer in our life without having to play out dramas and intrigues.

Quieting the mind is essential. Entertain joyful thoughts about those experiences you genuinely want to have and enjoy.

MEDITATION

Meditation is a deep state of relaxation that trains the mind and supports an inward focus. Practice anywhere to tune in to alternate states of consciousness, receive messages, visions, answers to questions, and explore the unseen and unknown. Here are simple suggestions for beginning a practice of meditation.

- Initiate SEEN.
- Choose a specific location to meditate—preferably not where you work, sleep or exercise.
- Make sure you will not be disturbed by phones, visitors, animals, etc.
- Early mornings are a great time to meditate—the world is quieter; energy is fresh and the mind uncluttered.
- Set aside a specific time to meditate each day.
- Place candles and other spiritual objects in the room to help you feel at ease.
- Find a way and position that works for you. Try sitting, lying, eyes closed, eyes opened as different ways to meditate.
- Once the mind quiets, put all your attention to the feet and then slowly move your consciousness up the body (including your internal organs).
- Enjoy the stillness.
- Once your meditation is complete, spend 2-3 minutes feeling grateful for the opportunity to practice and your mind's ability to focus.
- Read books, go online and use CD's to assist in learning more about meditation.

Insights may be intuitive or an inexplicable sudden gift of spirit. They can be triggered by a dream or a thought, come to you in meditation or while walking or sleeping at a Sacred Place. The sound of a bird's call, the appearance of an animal or the words of someone else floating on the air can be the portal through which you discern your purpose, life's work, future, or deeper identity.

ASKING FOR ASSISTANCE

Beings in other dimensions are available to help and requesting assistance is our responsibility. Walking, sitting, standing, or lying— practice and use this example of how to connect with the invisible world and ask for assistance.

- Initiate SEEN.
- Call in your higher power (Christ, Goddess, God, angels, allies, ancestors, ascended masters, healing masters, Eternal Divine Self, guardians, saints, etc.) and ask them to be present with you.
- State that your heart is open and invite your higher power to come rest in your heart—enter your energy field—speak to you through your mind or show you symbols or visions.
- Silently name everything you are grateful for in your life, all that you love, enjoy, and cherish. Be thorough and take as long as needed.
- Silently name all you are confident about in your life, those things you know you will bring to fruition—the creations or dreams already set in motion that you know will happen.
- Make requests for what you desire to draw into your life—healing, awareness, well-being, change, enlightenment, clarity, etc.
- Feel the nutrients of the earth and the essence of what is desired flowing into the energy field and body. Direct the energy to any part of the body, mind or spirit that would benefit from deep nurturing and healing.
- Images, colors, or words may be given. You may suddenly get a bright idea or see an option you overlooked previously.

Information comes to us like puzzle pieces we eventually assemble. Allow the pieces to be given—the complete answer may not appear all at once.

DIVINING TECHNIQUES

Before entering a Sacred Place, intend to connect deeply.

Sacred Places invite us to explore divining techniques (develop our inner knowing and psychic abilities). Divination is the ability to foresee, gain insight into a question or situation or be inspired. For thousands of years, diviners have worked with deep sensitivities and a heightened sense of awareness, used divination tools, read signs or omens, and spoken with supernatural beings. Divination practices vary throughout the world by culture, religion, and individual proclivities.

Your ability to discover, foresee or predict something, as if super-naturally, requires a shift in focus and the use of abilities we all have. You may have more finely tuned abilities in certain areas and it is practical and recommended to explore various ways of divining.

Trust the information you receive. Ask to be shown—and shown more clearly.

Presented here are some powerful divining techniques for an Integrative Archaeologist. If you feel drawn to know more about divining techniques, or feel you have a gift that needs support and development, acquire books, stream online, or take an interactive class to develop your intuition. If you feel confident, just dive in—trusting you will be guided and given the information you are seeking at Sacred Places.

Work with several methods to find your strengths and identify your comfort zone. The material here is intended to familiarize the reader with tools used by Integrative Archaeologists. It is not within the scope of this book to transmit in-depth training.

DOWSING AT SACRED PLACES

PENDULUM FOR DOWSING*

Dowsing has been around as long as humans and is a type of divination or clairvoyant ability. A dowser can search for anything by projecting an intent or question and receiving confirmation or non-confirmation through their dowsing devices or bodily felt sense. We already know the answer and the emanations from our body and nervous system motivate the movements of the dowsing device to provide the response. Dowsing enables us to out-picture our inner knowing.

Dowsing devices such as Y-shaped or L-shaped rods, pendulums or the body itself can be used to locate ground water, lost objects, gemstones, buried metals, ores, oil, to answer questions, measure chakras, vortices, portals and specific energies at Sacred Places.

Right and left-brain integration is a benefit of dowsing; it demands that we remain open intuitively as well as alert rationally. Exploration of our inner environment as well as the outer environment can be accomplished with dowsing as we tune in to the world of intuition, feeling and the sacred. Following are a few suggestions outlining how dowsing can be used at Sacred Places:

- Communicate or receive guidance from angels, allies, ancestors, guardians, and beings at Sacred Places.
- Find places where the energy field alters human consciousness, power spots and vortex sites.
- Locate underground water lines, springs, high energy places.
- Find ley lines and the directions in which their energy flows.
- Determine whether a ley line or water line has a positive or negative effect on what lies above or over it.
- Identify locations where events took place.
- Identify locations of healing.
- Find ancient ceremonial locations.
- Locate portals, inter-dimensional doorways, and gateways.
- Have specific questions answered.

BODY DOWSING

Below are techniques that use the body and do not require the use of a device. Practice by asking the body questions as you go through your day. For example: Should I invest time in this project? Should I go for a walk right now? Is it wise to let this person become a friend? Is the new project I am being offered beneficial for me? Is this relationship ideal? You can ask the body anything, anytime.

Listening, being silent, feeling the sensations in the body, allowing yourself to be led to a spot or location is a kind of dowsing done without a device. When traveling to Sacred Places, having this skill in place will be most valuable. Body dowsing can be relied upon to answer questions and give direction.

The body can be used as a pendulum that will sway one way for yes and another way for no (back and forth or side to side).

- Stand and place the feet hip width apart.
- Close the eyes and ask the body to show you its yes and then, show you its no.
- Do this every time you decide to body dowse, since the direction of movement could change.
- Ask your body a question to which you know the answer is yes: is my name_____?
- Ask the body a question to which you know the answer is no.
- Continue with the question to which you desire an answer from the body.
- Trust the answer you receive.
- Thank the body.

THUMB AND INDEX FINGER DOWSING

- Create a loop with the thumb and index finger.
- Place the other thumb and index finger together in the loop and connect these two loops creating a chain with these fingers.

- Ask what is yes and try to pull the fingers apart.
- Ask what is no and repeat the process of trying to pull the fingers apart.
- In one instance, your fingers will lock tightly so you cannot get them apart. In the other instance one loop will slip through the other, separating the chain.
- To confirm this method is working, ask questions you know the answers to.
- Ask the questions you would like to have answered.
- Trust the answer.
- Thank the body. Easy!

RUBBING THE FINGERS TOGETHER DOWSING

Gently rub the thumb and index fingers together. Close your eyes and relax. You may experience a silky smoothness, roughness, up and down, side-to-side or another signal as you:

- Ask to be shown a yes.
- Ask to be shown a no.
- Clear your mind.
- Ask your guides and allies to assist.
- Check responses by asking questions you already know answers to.
- Ask the questions you would like answered.
- Trust the answer.
- Thank the body.

DREAMING AT SACRED PLACES

Stories of dreaming at Sacred Places appear in legends about sacred wells in Ireland, Scotland and England, where a goddess was the overseer. Dreamers sought answers to relationship questions: When will I marry? Will I find true love? Should I remain in this relationship? The goddess of the well would answer the question through a dream.

Water symbolizes the subconscious or super-conscious mind, what is hidden. Dreaming at Sacred Places, particularly near water, is highly recommended as a way to gain insight, determine next steps and clarify your current life situations.

Find a quiet place to sleep and dream undisturbed. Program and direct the path of your dreams:

- Initiate SEEN.
- Focus on an intention for your dreaming.
- Formulate a clear question and use the following statements to program your dreams:
  - I program my dreams to acquire information about my next career steps.
  - I program my dreams to show me how to heal.
  - I program my dreams to reveal information about my relationship with_____

EXTRA-SENSORY PERCEPTION

Beyond the five acknowledged sense we are most accustomed to using is another set of senses we all possess. Due to lack of use, we sometimes fail to activate these sense or doubt and mistrust them when they operate automatically. For some, it is remembering or relearning to utilize all we have been given – to operate at full capability. Extra Sensory Perception involves awareness of information about events external to the self—information gained through the senses and not deducible from previous experience.

Have you ever thought of someone and almost instantly received a phone call or piece of mail from them? Had a dream or vision about something or someone to find it comes true? Do you know something about the past that you did not experience or live through? Been told you are reading someone else's thoughts? Have you had a premonition about the future that materialized? If so, you have been operating in the realm of Extra Sensory Perception. ESP.

ESP is the ability to acquire information about the world around you without relying upon the normal senses of sight, touch, taste, hearing, and smell.

There are several types of extrasensory perception. The major types are telepathy, clairvoyance, precognition, retrocognition, mediumship, and psychometry.

Often referred to as the "sixth sense", ESP is not bound by the limits of time and space. Does the information come through mind, body, gut, heart? Maybe all are involved.

The practice of Integrative Archaeology is greatly enhanced and supported by the development and use of our ESP.

TELEPATHY: "I SPEAK AND LISTEN"

Thought transference is the easiest way to describe telepathy. Practice and you will be surprised at how often you are already using telepathy to communicate. Animals are highly telepathic, and they like to receive images rather than words. Babies, little beings that are new to our world, have their full telepathic abilities intact. Engage a baby in telepathic communication—and watch their face light up; they may even start laughing. Here are some telepathic messages we can use in our everyday encounters.

- I recognize you.
- I honor you.
- You are greatly loved.
- I love you.
- You are beautiful and brilliant!
- I am so happy you are here.
- You excel in all you undertake.
- You are a gift to the world.

Telepathy can be used to send messages at any time to anyone. Practice sending loving and uplifting messages to friends and business associates. Before going into a meeting, send messages of love and good wishes and your intentions for beneficial outcomes for everyone. Become aware of telepathic messages being sent to you.

CLAIRVOYANCE: "I SEE"

Clear seeing or vision is the nature of clairvoyance, including the ability to see the aura or energy body of a person, place, or thing. This type of seeing does not emanate from the physical eyes, but from an inner sight. Practice this with a partner who can present questions. Below are two ways to access clairvoyant abilities. Practice with each and see what is comfortable for you.

EXAMPLE #1

- Initiate SEEN.
- Close eyes and focus inward. Bring your attention to the area at the back of the head or base of the skull.
- Imagine the area behind the forehead on the inside of the head as a clear white movie screen. Some people like to imagine the screen somewhere in front of the forehead outside the physical body. Either way will work.
- Ask or have someone else pose a question.
- Allow images generated at the back of the skull to be projected on the forehead. These images might include objects, colors, names, words, numbers, scenes and may have meaning to you or the questioner. You may be given a series of images.
- Describe and speak them.
- You or your partner will have interpretations of these images. Have fun with this.

EXAMPLE #2

- Initiate SEEN.
- Close the eyes and look upward, accessing the area at the top of the head.
- Imagine you can open this area (known as the seventh or crown chakra) and create a funnel-shaped conduit that spans out from the top of the head. In this way, we open to Source.
- Ask questions and wait for responses. Images, words or thoughts, colors, shapes, phrases or objects may appear.
- The art of interpreting the images develops over time and through experience.

CLAIRAUDIENCE: "I HEAR"

Clairaudience is likely to be most appealing to those of us who think in words. This is not hearing with our physical ears. Try the following exercise:

- Initiate SEEN.
- Focus your attention inside the head.

- Direct the focus of your hearing to an area above the ears.
- Words, sounds or other types of language are experienced as an inner dialogue—like talking to the self.
- Write or speak what you hear.

Here is one of my (many) experiences with Clairaudience.

Sedona, AZ - 2009

It was a chilly November morning and I was called upon to take a woman out to a remote location in the desert where there is a cave up in the rocks. Accustomed to the site, we easily made our way out along the dirt roads and desert path and up the side of a hill toward the cave.

As I looked at the ledge, we would have to transit to reach the cave by leaning our bodies, chest first, into rock with a fall of several hundred feet below, I decided "no." Did the ledge appear too narrow and the drop much further than ever before? It looked to me as if the ledge was less than half the width, I remembered it being. What was going on?

"Let's go around the hill, maybe we can get in from the other side."

Although I had visited many times it did not feel safe to go out on the ledge and take another person, completely inexperienced, with me. This was a big and important journey for my guest, and I could sense her disappointment. I wanted to instill some hope that we could still access the cave without engaging in death-defying feats. I had no idea if there was another entrance on the far side, but willing to try.

Along the way we found some sweet areas where alcoves and overhangs protected the remains of Sinagua or Anasazi housing. This was new information for me, I had not ventured in this direction before. At the end of our journey was a huge rock; likely the ceiling of the cave was somewhere below. There was no path around the rock and climbing up it looked like it would terminate in another extremely high ledge. I could see no way we would be able to gain access from this side.

"There is no way to get there from here." I announced, dashing any hope she had of finally entering the mystical cave.

I remarked on the amazing find of the ruins along the way, "we gained some excellent insight on this journey and got to see hidden places." She was not nearly as excited as I was about these finds, her dream was now lost.

As we made our way back across what was partially a path, and partially a bush whacking experience, the voices of two young people, maybe teenagers, boy and girl, drifted up, a gentle backdrop to our conversation. I noticed this as we walked and talked but made no mention of it – the laughter from below and light joyful conversation running right alongside our conversation.

I kept looking down, as the two people had to be quite nearby, on a path or in an area just below where we walked. The words could not be deciphered, but the gentle tones of laughter sounded like two people in love in a heightened experience.

Once we were on the main path down the hill, I looked up again hoping to spot them, but figured we would come across their car as there was only one dirt road to park on. Nothing. No other cars, motorcycles, jeeps, or other conveyances anywhere in sight.

"Did you hear that conversation going on as we walked back along the path?" I asked. "I wonder where the people are or how they got up here, there is no car." She looked at me. "What conversation, what people? I didn't hear or see anyone."

CLAIRALIENCE: "I SMELL"

Our sense of smell is a magical time machine, connecting us with pasts into antiquity and the wealth of information that lies there. Smell, scent or olfaction is an ancient sense embedded deep within our primal response system. The right aroma can evoke vivid, whole body sensations that help us recognize life partners and choose friends. Smell assists us to instantaneously recall memories and can transport us back in time to experience a scene from the past.

Have you ever heard anyone say: Every time I smell _____, I remember _____? Smells trigger memory more than hearing or seeing. The smell of a ripe peach can bring us back to a summer day in an orchard long ago. The scent of a pot of soup cooking on the stove wafting its aroma throughout the house may bring a sense of peace, nurturing, happiness, or wellbeing. The scent of candles and incense transports us inside a cathedral to an ancient ceremony.

A sniff of something on the air and we suddenly remember events we have forgotten for years, maybe lifetimes. These smells influence our moods, health, and work performance.

Using our sense of smell at Sacred Places is an excellent way to connect more deeply. A rock, tree, plant, the earth itself—all have a scent—and that scent carries upon it the memories of times past and dimensions beyond this one.

Place a drop of essential oil in the palm of the hand, rub the hands together and cup the hands over the nose and sniff the essence of the plant.

Clairalience signals us about people and events and is a means of communication from the spirit world to us. Messages of smell are some- times spontaneous and we can also ask for this type of information.

- Initiate SEEN.
- Use essential oils as a transport system.
- Focus your attention on the heart center.
- Ask for any scents to be presented to you that are relevant to your exploration.

Midday, we sat in a circle under the trees above Machu Picchu. A light drizzle sparked the landscape – the group was meditating and tuning into the site and themselves. Our lunch awaited at the Sanctuary Lodge; the kitchen would be closing shortly, and it was raining.

We made our descent through the city gate, down the center steps in the rain. Lifted by the slight wind, my thin rain poncho required constant batting down so I could see the steps. The smell of peppermint lifesavers hung in the air and I figured there must be someone nearby eating them.

I did not look up, around or sideways—my concentration point was the rain-drenched stone steps and getting down them safely. A while later, the peppermint lifesaver smell again wafted into my zone and I thought for a split second how there must be someone walking close behind me – certainly, there was no one to either side or in front.

Turning right I continued across flat ground toward the exit and was enveloped in the strong smell of peppermint lifesavers and finally realized this was something drifting through in the olfactory senses—contact from another dimension.
I asked myself who this might be and immediately I saw my grandmother's green 1952 Chevy with a package of peppermint lifesavers on the plastic covered front bench seat of the car. Emotion welled up as I realized what was happening—contact from my dear grandmother.

TEMPLE OF THE SUN, MACHU PICCHU, PERU

The use of essential oils at Sacred Places is recommended. Use essential oils from plants native to the areas visited. The plants from which they were extracted carry the earth's memory. Use the oils during meditation, spirit communication or any time a deeper connection is desired. Place a drop of essential oil on the forehead or heart.

CLAIRCOGNIZANCE: "I KNOW"

Did you ever just know something? Dozens of these small enlightenments guide us through our days and support us to make decisions—like which line to stand in at the grocery store. Our knowing may facilitate a quicker checkout, put us next to someone we need to meet or in earshot of a conversation we need to overhear for our own benefit. We simply know where to be. We do not question this type of knowing.

CLAIRGUSTANCE: "I TASTE"

A flavor or taste on the tip of the tongue reminds us of a person or event. We can ask to be given the taste of a thing, some place or event and it will trigger a broader sense of the experience.

CLAIRSENTIENCE: "I FEEL"

Sensitivity and silence enhance our feeling abilities. Being in touch with how something feels in the body is an excellent indicator. A clairsentient psychic may take the hand of a client for a moment to connect and receive impressions—to feel what is going on.

- Initiate SEEN.
- Ask a question or have someone else ask.
- Notice how it feels—scan the body for any signals.
- What does your body tell you?

PSYCHOMETRY: "I TOUCH"

The hands are the sensory system used in psychometry—we touch an object to receive impressions. Metal objects, like jewelry, are excellent to practice with as the metal holds the vibration of wearers. Antique jewelry may have had more than one owner—see if you can tap into the person who originally acquired the piece. Try this with other objects too—an article of clothing, a pen, artifacts. It is best to practice with objects that are not your own or objects of antiquity that have a history to reveal.

Practicing with another person can provide valuable responses and comments. Exchange impressions you receive from the objects you are examining and clarify each other's findings. An outing to an antique shop can be fun. There you may have the opportunity to interact with several different objects.

- Initiate SEEN.
- Hold the object in your hand(s), close your eyes and see what images, words, or other information comes to you.

- Speak it out loud if you are working with a partner or write it down if you are working alone.

If you are in a location where touching the object is not possible, place the palm of your hand(s) a few inches or more away from the object, close your eyes, relax, and breathe. Connect with the object through that little heart chakra at the center of the palm of the hand. The impressions you receive will offer clues and entire stories or events for your consideration.

ASTRAL PROJECTION: "I TRAVEL"

The ability to separate the astral (spirit) body from the physical body and fly or travel to other locations is known as astral projection. We leave ordinary reality and enter multidimensional reality to travel. Deep meditative states and altered states enhance this ability. It is best to be guided through the process of astral travel.

RETROCOGNITION: "I REMEMBER"

Retrocognition is a sudden experience or knowledge of past events that could not have been inferred or learned by normal means. You might be left wondering: Did it happen in a dream? Did the psyche travel backward to get the information? We can investigate and perceive the past:

- Initiate SEEN.
- Close your eyes and shift your focus to inside the head.
- Look with the inner eye in every direction and ask which direction to focus on to see the past.
- Images, colors, numbers, or entire scenes may be given. If what you are seeing is not clear, ask for greater clarity, a sharper image.

PRECOGNITION: "I KNEW IT"

Precognition is knowing or being aware of something to take place in the future.

This can happen spontaneously. Practice looking into the future with this exercise:

- Initiate SEEN.
- Close the eyes and shift your focus to inside your head.
- Look with the inner eye in every direction, asking which direction to focus on to see the future.
- Allow the images to flow in, collect them, write them down or speak them.

Golden morning sun streams across the rooftop of my hotel in Lima and I am watching peacocks strut and giant turtles crawl about. Birds of all descriptions visit feeders perched higher up. A cat saunters by on her own mission.

Half an hour later I am at the front door greeting my driver, Leonardo, who will take me to the Sacred City of Caral which traditional archaeologists claim to be a 5,000 year old metropolis representing the oldest known civilization in the Americas. It may be older.

Leonardo is a kind and joyful man and I ask him if we can get a coffee to go, forgetting that "to go" is not a concept that has any relevance to the Peruvians or many other cultures. No one is in no rush and enjoy a respite for coffee or tea as an opportunity to visit with whomever their companion might be or whomever they meet at the café.

Leonardo parks the car and walks up a flight of stairs to what could almost be someone's home and take a table near the window overlooking a small square away from the main areas of Lima. Pastries are brought out and we talk a bit about Caral in Spanish with a little English spliced in. He has made the trip before and, he notes, it will take us three hours or so along the Pan-American Highway to get there.

We drive across the visually bland landscape until it appears there are dunes that could be mountains stretching a far distance from the Pacific Ocean. We go from paved road to dirt track lined with white painted rocks drawing us closer to the site.

The photos I have seen of the site are compelling and I have known of its existence for some time. Purposely, I have avoided reading about the site, I like to see what a site can tell me, unencumbered by known findings and theories. Silently, I recite my prayer to the guardians of the ancient city requesting entry and whatever the guardians, ancestors, and site itself may have to share with me.

CARAL, PERU

We approach the site and I see newer service buildings have been constructed with shiny bamboo-like poles. The entry fee is 21 Sols (about $6.00) whether you go through the site alone or with a group. A whole group pays 21 sols and one person pays 21 sols Leonardo declines coming along.

There is no way to enter alone—a guide is assigned to each person or group and the guide walks you along the dusty paths that are also lined with stones – although not painted white. From these pathways I can look at the structures but that is as close as I will be able to get. This was an arid, dry desert with not a plant in site.

My visit to Caral in Peru was one of being an onlooker—guided along a path and seeing the archaeological evidence in the distance. It appeared there would be no place to sit, stop, lay down on the earth or meditate. Here, everyone must have a guide who tells you about the site and what they have been trained to say.

My custom is to take time—lots of it. Usually I find one or several spots to sit or lie on the earth and connect. The question of accessibility for an Integrative Archaeologist is brought forward. What if you find yourself in a situation like this, a viewer and listener with no easy way to make your own determinations? After travelling such a long distance to get to such a site, I want to have more of an experience to draw upon.

It is pointed out by the guide that pyramids were ceremonial sites, flat on top. The stones were held together with clay and all was painted yellow – one of the structures the north facing section was painted white. There are six pyramids in various stages of excavation – a project that has been going on for eighteen years. The main pyramid has five layers of construction beneath it, each one built upon the last. People lived here, community life and ceremonies took place. I listen to these basic facts, all the time scanning and feeling into the earth.

It was not until I reached a portion of the path where I could look down into the Supe Valley and see lush green that there was some relief from the gray/brown sands. The river runs through the valley when the runoff from the Andes flows and agriculture took place in the distant past as it does now. No one lived in the valley, they all lived up above, I am told.

As I move along the dusty path, half listening to the guide, I sense many ceremonial places and see two fire rings of stone with ventilation below. The ventilation, I learned later, is a duct system that flowed air from one fire ring to another to keep the fires burning. Not everyone could enter the Sacred Places, the guide remarks. several feet away.

A seven-foot-tall monolith stood within a circle and I stopped there for a while. The guide noted this was called the monolith Huanca and archaeologists believe that this monolith was used for astronomical and ceremonial purposes, and for determining the time of day.

Closing my eyes, I see many people gathered around the monolith in concentric circles. Were they wearing white or standing in a white light? I could not tell as the vision was fleeting. Some of the participants wore tall headpieces with feathers and there were colorful birds sitting on the shoulders of a few. Something like a hum rose *from the group, voice harmonics, shared sonic field? No words, just harmonics. That was it – just a glimpse, encased in a kind of mist or fog.*

I found a low rock wall that had obviously been built as part of the pathway and was not a part of the site and rested there for a few minutes. The guide sits down too, several feet away.

I close my eyes, breath in through the top of my head, out through the heart. My hands cover my chest as this position allows me to immediately sink into a meditative state. Right away, I hear the music of what sounds like a flute, the sounds stop and start a few times like bad reception on the radio.

"Escuchas musica"? "Do you hear the music"?

I ask the thin, wiry guide. He furrows his brow and looks from side to side as my eyes scan the entire visible area. I know I am the only person here today.

"No musica aqui." "No music here." He pronounces, looking at me curiously.

I close my eyes again and the music continues, flute and some other instrument occasionally, probably no longer than a minute—then silence. An image of Tiahanaco's Sun Gate appears. What could that have to do with this place?

SUN GATE, DETAIL, TIAHUANACO, BOLIVA

Years later I would read about a gourd found in the area with a carved image of the "staff god" who appears at the sun gate in Tiahuanaco. A figure who holds a staff in one hand and snake or lightning bolt or another taff in the other–appearing in Andean iconography.

I open my eyes and think the best way to access the site might be through objects in the museum in Lima – if there are any – or a book.

It is hot and I am tired and facing the drive back to Lima, another three or more hours. As I walk back toward the entry, I silently call upon the ancestors to give me any messages they may have and I immediately hear "make love, not war." Was it John Lennon who said that in modern times? Nevertheless, I will write it down in my journal once I am back in the car.

I will learn later that no weapons of war or evidence of conflict or injuries were found at the site, Traditional archaeologists believe this was a peaceful society living for the pleasure of life itself.

Finally, I reach the entry and Leonardo is engaged in a conversation with the site monitors standing under a tarp with an array of books on sale. Carting books back is a heavy proposition, but often the books are only available at the site location or within the county, so I have learned to buck up and cart them home. I purchase a couple books, but it will be some time after my return home that I look at the books and have a chance to read a couple articles about the site.

It is then that I will learn of the 32 flutes made of condor and pelican bones that were discovered at the site. Cornets, 37 small trumpet-like instruments made of deer and llama bones, were also discovered. Decorations on the instruments include engraved bird-faced snakes, a double head comprising a bird and snake, monkeys and supernatural birds combining features of some other creatures such as felines or monkeys. Two anthropomorphic figures were also carved into the instruments.

These were found in a circular area presumed to be a gathering /ceremonial space.

I would go to Caral again, explore much more of the surrounding area. Stay for some days and absorb more of what this amazing site has to impart.

11

THE ROLE OF PRACTICAL SHAMANISM

AVALON NEAR GLASTONBURY N SOMERSET, ENGLAND

STONE CIRCLE NEAR SLIGO, IRELAND

THE ROLE OF PRACTICAL
SHAMANISM

*Shamanism is an integration of the physical and spiritual realms of existence
and is based on the knowledge that all life is interconnected.*

The terms shaman and shamanism are overused and improperly allocated to medicine people and other practitioners in various cultures. Specific practices by shamans and other medicine people at Sacred Places are endlessly varied — originating from different cultures and belief systems worldwide.

Shamanism is an earth based spiritual practice that cuts across all faiths and creeds and reaches into the depths of ancestral memory. Shamanism was practiced long before organized religion came into being. The belief systems, symbolism and cosmology contain gods, totems and beings who take different forms based on their cultural place of origin.

Practical shamanism requires the development of sensitivity, heightened states of awareness and a connection to all life. To be able to enter multidimensional reality and commune with spirits at Sacred Places, it is necessary to embrace a shamanic awareness of the world in which we live—to respect and nurture all life.

*Practical shamanism establishes a foundation for
multidimensional awareness and communication.*

Practical shamanism is a way of being and seeing supported by a deep sensitivity to the Self and the Earth and a willingness to connect with and consciously use the energy of the cosmos. This foundation enables the Integrative Archaeologist to explore the invisible realms of existence. The basis of practical shamanism as outlined in this book relates to connecting with Sacred Places and the beings inhabiting them. As we nurture our sensitivity, we solidify the platform for our experience of this and other realms of existence.

> *He (the Shaman) is a self-reliant explorer of the endless mansions*
> *of a magnificent hidden universe.* Michael Harner

The shaman is a human bridge between the unseen realms of guiding spirits and this world—present time—Now. Shamanic practice requires full presence in the Now, as you cannot be a bridge to a place you are not present in.

The word shaman originated among the Siberian Tungus (Evenks) and literally means s/he who knows. Shamanism predated Christianity as the dominant religious practice for humanity reaching as far back as 2.6 million years ago. Today, the word shaman is liberally applied to medicine people of many indigenous cultures throughout the world. Some of the defining skills shaman's practice and have been credited with include:

- Divination
- The interpretation of dreams and visions
- Healing
- Astral projection
- Enlightenment
- The ability to contact the spirit world while in an altered state of consciousness
- Acting as an intermediary or messenger between the human world and the spirit worlds
- Knowing the entire universe to be alive and interconnected mending of the soul to restore the physical body
- Acquiring solutions to bring positive effects to their community
- Bringing guidance for others
- Restoring balance to people and environments
- Birthing transcendent energies

Totem animals figure strongly in the practice of shamanism and it is believed that all animals bring teachings. A shaman can imitate and/or take the form of a totem animal during a ritual or ceremony. Teachings of a totem animal may become part of the shaman's medicine—that which is shared with others. The ancient use of other totem items such as rocks or crystals is common among shamans as they are believed to have an animating spirit and special powers.

ANIMAL MESSENGERS

During the course of a ceremony, meditation or intentional journey be aware of any animals that make an appearance. Also, as you go through your day, just notice if a particular bird or animal appears. They come as messengers and are often responding to your questions or prayers. There are several fine books on Animal Totems and their meanings; become familiar with the unique messages they bring. Many meanings may be assigned to each animal, take from them what your intuition tells you is most relevant.

One April morning, I was in my office talking with a friend who was visiting. Looking in her direction I saw an animal slip over the rock wall at the edge of the patio. I thought 'javelina' but then noticed the grace with which the animal moved. I stood up and moved closer and saw an adolescent black bear. Bears do make it into town, but it's a rare occurrence. As she walked closer, she stood on hind legs to sniff a flower basket hanging in a tree outside my window and I took her picture. She walked along to the porch where she sniffed many other flowers on the screened in porch and then made her way out into the field. I later learned she crossed the four-lane road, visited the Whole Foods dumpster, and finally showed up at the school (where they evacuated the children) and finally went out into the forest. I was so grateful she made it to safety before someone fearful of her harmed her. She had the sweetest energy.

Bears are considered the embodiment of spiritual power and physical strength. Although rarely seen, bears are often called into ceremonies for their healing powers – they ingest plants and herbs for their own healing. It was believed bears would die each fall and come back to life in the spring, verifying their spiritual power over death, the power of resurrection and rebirth. We know that bears actually hibernate during the winter months. This is a time for them to seek spiritual realignment. Once they awaken from their long journey into the spirit world, they are greater in their spirit and lesser in body. The bear stands erect to embrace the gifts of Father Sun, awakening, renewal.

This is just one perspective about the meaning and power of the bear, there are many. Read about the animals that come into your presence and learn the gifts they bring.

BEAR IN SEDONA

The first prophecies were the words of an oak, and that everyone who lived at that time found it rewarding enough to "listen to an oak or a stone, so long as it was telling the truth." Plato, *Phaedrus*

Some societies believe shamanic abilities are inherited and can be passed from generation to generation. Others believe shamans must be "called" to serve—apprenticing themselves to accomplished shamans. Others believe the shaman is naturally initiated.

Being struck by lightning, a personal psychological crisis, a near death experience or a serious illness can initiate the shaman. A shaman may be transported to the spirit world, experience a dismantling or dismemberment and then a reconstruction. Initiatory experiences may bring specific visions, imagery, or revelations of magical powers.

Many cultures had their shamanic practices wiped out with the spread of Christianity, as temples were destroyed, and ceremonies were outlawed. Campaigns against "witches," often orchestrated by the Catholic Inquisition wiped out European shamanism during the Middle Ages and Renaissance. Spanish colonization brought Christianity in its wake, instrumental in the destruction of local traditions. Medicine people were executed as "devil worshipers" in the Caribbean and Central and South America. The English Puritans in North America conducted periodic campaigns against individuals perceived to be witches.

Christian missionaries still, today, carry out attacks on shamanic practitioners in developing countries. Missionaries in the Amazon defaced historic petroglyphs just a few decades ago. The list goes on and the idea that my god is better than your god remains a prevalent theme causing death and destruction worldwide. Shamanism continues to survive in indigenous communities and other locations throughout the world.

COYOTE, SEDONA

STINGRAY /PUERTO PENASCO, MEXICO

Shamanic symbols, totem animals
who makes them appear to those who can read them?
we are doubtless - at once - the shaman and the animal

Driving out of town on my way to Mexico
an owl flew right to left in front of the car –
a symbol telling me that something from the unconscious, unseen
will come into awareness, make itself known – visible -
Present itself for examination

Later that same day in the warm salty sea treading barefoot toward land
I felt a strike so hard and a pain so loud I screamed out – do lobsters bite?
Something bit me!

Resort security identified the culprit immediately as "raya"
a shock to the system with an Impact so powerful, it can penetrate a wooden boat
my water shoes would not have saved me they said
so,I bore no guilt for not wearing them that day

Known for its fluidity of movement, agility, and the ability to lay low and camouflage itself
raya – the stingray - struck with its sting infusing me with its venom
my right big toe bled and clotted the sand with each step

The intense bleeding was good they told me - it takes the poison out
according to Hebrew tradition, the basis of our healing is always the shedding of blood
God never heals, never blesses, never arrests the action of evil apart from the shedding of blood.
Suddenly I am in the pyramids and ruins, cold, wet rock walls covered in moss
landing on a day when the past had already become the future
drinking from a vessel found only in museums
witnessing silent movies of pasts embedded in the vibration of the structures

finding there the stingray spines that clued archaeologists to the bloodletting rituals
performed by the ancient Maya at Tikal during the Hiatus period from 562 -695 AD

I left there in pursuit of hurry, under my own steam I moved on
following a trail of scattered breadcrumbs through the forest of my life
because in fact, something unseen, from the unconscious
did come up to bite me.
and it did not take me long to remember that this has happened before

right in front of me, in a flash I saw her, a miniature five-year-old goddess
wearing a brown and white cotton checked dress, framed in a garden hedge
overqualified for the job of revelations and practiced at silence and invisibility
holding the answer in the palm of her hand like a sparkling golden egg.

Luminous Antonia, 2007

ACCESSING SPIRIT WORLDS

Spiritual preparation for visits to Sacred Places is a matter of personal beliefs and preferences—there is no right way to do this. Devoting time and energy to an upcoming Sacred Place journey or ceremony does have a payoff—we position ourselves to receive the benefits we are seeking.

A shaman or medicine person takes time to prepare the body, mind and spirit for ceremonies and journeys to Sacred Places. The purpose of spiritual preparation is to amplify and sustain the vibration of our entire being. The vibration and frequency we hold is the magnet attracting what we desire, others and those in the unseen dimensions. Great care is taken to purify and enrich the being on all levels. When we take the time to prepare our whole being, communication with the spirit world and Sacred Places happens easily and effortlessly.

Preparation might include spending time with an elder who can initiate you into the ways of communicating with the spirit world. Teachings about offerings and ceremonies, customs, ancestors, rituals, and other dimensions are shared. Often, a journey to a Sacred Place is a rite of passage intended to reveal a spiritual or life direction. In our modern society, these traditions may be limited or non-existent.

There are none greater or less than you in all the worlds. Sam Tchakalian, Artist

Integrative Archaeologists may frame their journey and visit as a rite of passage or place it in any context they wish. You are encouraged and supported to contact the spirit world. Following are some examples of traditional ways of preparing for a spiritual journey:

- Meditating
- Fasting
- Elimination of alcohol and drug use
- Sensory deprivation
- Praying
- Journaling (including dream journaling)
- Reading inspirational books
- Becoming familiar and comfortable with solitude
- Reviewing the past and reasons for making the journey
- Contemplating the meaning of surrender
- Preparing the Self for a symbolic death and rebirth—the old Self dies, and we anticipate renewal through the birth of a new Self
- Singing and dancing
- Ritual practices
- Chanting and voice harmonics
- Ceremonial bathing (to cleanse physically and spiritually)
- Using altars or medicine bags before or during a journey
- Ceremonial fires

HOPI

Supernaturals known as kachinas
appearing as plants
animals
clouds
stars
and sky
side with Hopis to pull up corn from arid earth
bring clouds and rain
cure diseases

freezing March winds sweep across Hopi mesas at night
below ground
people
crushed together in kivas
hear rapping on the roof
announcing Kachinas
mud heads and clowns
throwing oranges, popcorn, and radishes to eager takers
wearing collars and clothing of tree branches
round the neck and wrist and ankles
stamping and chanting ancient rhythmic stories
calling through from a place long distant
in the underworld
as far away as timeless
shaking the earth
opening the heart
soothing the soul

in the morning
of the next day
all that can be seen is a line of kachinas
winding out of the village
along a dirt path
straw-like weeds frozen from winter
teardrops recalling some other past

Luminous Antonio, 2022

SENSITIZE

I want you to learn a new way of using your mind that liberates you from "facts"
and "beliefs" by focusing on your own direct, moment-to-moment experience. This is
where your real power resides; this is the way to wisdom. Christian de Quincey

An inward focus is crucial to personal fulfillment and to communicating with invisible worlds. Relaxing and stabilizing the physical body, quieting the mind, and centering in the heart (SEEN) prepares and supports the Integrative Archaeologist to connect.

TUNE IN

Insight into and communion with the unseen, other dimensional realities and the beings inhabiting them is at the core of Integrative Archaeology. Tuning in to higher frequencies requires an inward focus and the elimination of distractions.

Our world is saturated with abundant, unfiltered incoming information and background noise from electronic devices. We have been conditioned to hook up to predominant cultural information sources that do us no good, do not add to our wellbeing and are often disturbing, fear-based, and detrimental to our health.

Streaming images and chatter flow through televisions, radios and other electronic media and spout off in almost every environment we enter. Channels provided by consensus reality dull the senses, instill unwanted programs, influence our thinking and feeling bodies and condition us to a fear-based existence. Captive in a kind of trance, dis- connected, the sounds of the earth, animals and plants and the messages of spirit are diminished or lost.

The need to be constantly entertained diminishes our ability to connect
with, be enlivened by, and in flow with the natural world.

There are other channels—channels emanating from an infinite domain of expanded consciousness. Silence opens us to higher thought and unlimited realms of information. Our inner knowing is strengthened. We can create and choose stories we want to tell ourselves—stories reflecting a reality experience we strongly desire to live out, free of fear, disease, and destruction.

Silence and listening tunes us into what stillness has to reveal. Our connection with ourselves, the natural world, our planet, and other people becomes the primary information source.

PRESENCE

Leave the mind vivid, without any constructions, just as it is. In the space
between old and new ideas, discover the natural, unfabricated, luminous and
knowing nature of the mind unaffected by thought. H.H. Dalai Lama

We receive more from life and relationships when we locate ourselves in the Now. The subtle energies and beings at Sacred Places require our full presence. In any situation where full presence is required, alcohol and drug use is not recommended.

*Release any psychological assessment, processing, thinking of the
past or future or other distracting mental activities.*

Land, waters, rocks, temples—whatever exists before, beneath, or around us is alive and vibrating with life force. Use the Heart-Opening Breath to clear the mind if it becomes cluttered with thoughts, assessments, and ideas.

CLOSE YOUR EYES

When we simply close the eyes to eliminate visual data and distractions, our inner focus is made active. Look up to the crown area of the head or focus on the area between the eyebrows and slightly above.

BREATHE

Exhale fully. The breath is automatically pulled into the body, filling the abdomen and chest. Deep breathing relaxes, centers, and connects us to the earth. Send out a vibration of love to everything and everyone around you.

SILENCE

Let us be silent, that we may hear the whispers of the gods. Ralph Waldo Emerson

Silence allows us to drop deeply into ourselves. When we eliminate speech and other sounds, we experience heightened awareness in all our other senses. Move your focus out of the head and into the heart. Silence opens the receptivity mode.

Silence is a multidimensional prayer, supporting our inner knowing and divining abilities.

LISTEN

Listen with the entire body. Listening to the sounds of birds, wind, trees, animals, people, and our footsteps on the earth allows us to consciously merge with the rhythms of the universe and become part of nature. Listening can be cultivated through silence and meditation.

BODILY FELT SENSE

*Check in with the body periodically and see what messages it
is putting forth. Honor the wisdom of the body.*

Our bodies are accurate sensing devices. Take time to scan the body and notice any areas of tingling, stiffness, pain, or other signals. Focus your attention inward:

- Bring your attention to the toes, then the feet.
- See into and feel the entire body—move your consciousness upward from the feet through the entire body, including the organs.
- Notice any areas of tightness, pain, etc.

- Does the body want to lie down, sit, or stand?
- Is there a feeling of exhilaration, tiredness, strength?
- Any aches, stiffness, or holding?
- Become aware of and tuned to the body's signals.

Interpretations about what these signals mean are left to the individual. Each of us carries unique pieces of a much larger puzzle; each of us will see, hear, and feel vastly different things. Every piece is important.

LET GO

When we believe things are a certain way and will remain so, we block the flow of new information and possibilities. Release the overlays of history, legend and interpretations, assumptions, and conditioning. These are someone else's findings. Let go of any preconceived ideas based on what has been read or heard. Allow Sacred Places to reveal themselves. What you see, intuit and experience will be unique and will tie into your life, dreams, and purpose.

TRUST

Trust may be the single most important element of any exploration into the invisible realms of life and Sacred Places. Integrative Archaeologists acquire information based on a heartfelt sense, visions, feelings, intuition, dreams, and personal connections made with ancient and prehistoric Sacred Places and cultures. Completely trust your insights and recognitions.

Don't worry, what is yours will come to you. Anthony Rossi, Father

OPEN YOUR HEART

Use the Heart-Opening Breath. Focus your consciousness in the heart and move slowly and softly to support the vulnerability of the open heart.

BECOME CHILDLIKE

Approach Sacred Places as a child might—openhearted, in wonder and enthusiastic to make discoveries. Ask to be shown and made aware of anything the site or guardians want to share.

BE RECEPTIVE

Receptivity is critical in welcoming new information. Staying open to what is presented and what you intuit supports the continued flow of information. Should you experience discomfort or an uncomfortable moment, stay with it and be willing to discover and receive what the experience has to show you.

OPEN YOUR HANDS

Opening the hands is a gesture of receptivity and willingness. There are little heart chakras in the palms of the hands. Maybe you have seen paintings or pictures of saints or holy people beaming light from the hands? Opening the hands with the palms facing forward enables us to beam our healing light out through the center of the hand and fingertips. Cast a path of light ahead of you, announcing your approach. This posture enables sensory information to gather and penetrate; it enhances our ability to connect and receive.

WALK SOFTLY

Consider each footstep a prayer.

Our feet are part of our multi-sensory system, and it is our feet that connect with the earth as we approach and explore Sacred Places. This is a practice to integrate anytime you are walking on the earth. It is particularly useful walking up hills or mountains:

- Slow your pace.
- Become aware of the heel touching the earth first, then the toe.
- As the left foot touches the earth, inhale and draw in the energy of the earth, the light.
- Flow this light through the body, revitalizing, renewing and restoring all parts of the being.
- As the right foot touches the earth, heel to toe, exhale and release any old, tired energy from the body. The earth receives this old energy and can use it (as it is not judged as good or bad) to revitalize itself. A healing exchange is created by this action.

CONNECT WITH THE EARTH

The shamanic practice of merging mind, body and spirit with the Earth's vibration opens a pathway for the direct flow of energy, feelings and healing, opening the Self to deep awareness.

Primary to our exploration of Sacred Places is making a connection with the earth. The earth is the keeper of great wisdom, renewal and healing and we can practice this connection anytime, anyplace in the world.

- Initiate SEEN.
- Lie face down, on your back or sit on the earth.
- Focus on the Heart-Opening Breath.
- Feel the earth beneath you, breathing with you.
- Experience your body as weighing a million pounds, sinking into the earth.
- Merge your energy field and body with that of the earth and relax into the wellbeing that is available.

ALTERED STATES

Mystics and shamans, among others, consider altered states a necessary discipline in their quest for the divine, truth, or reality. Our ordinary waking awareness is only one aspect of consciousness and viewing our lives from this single-point perspective can limit our field of vision and operation.

It is not necessary for the Integrative Archaeologist to seek altered states of awareness through plant medicine. Sensitivity to the Self and environment will produce an altered state automatically.

As visitors to Sacred Places we may experience a kind of altered state, a shift in awareness or consciousness. Naturally induced altered states take many forms, but most commonly, we may find ourselves in a partial dreaming and waking state. We may be unable or unwilling to speak, feel dizzy, hot or cold, enter a trance-like state, experience a shift in focus of our attention, become disoriented, or relaxed into a previously unknown peaceful state.

Our life experience is enriched by entering altered states— other planes of existence become known as we travel backwards and forwards in time.

Altered states open us to visions, voices, or sounds, stimulation of the chakras, out-of-body experiences, speaking in tongues, psychic phenomena, trances, ecstasy, communication with other beings, and feelings of union with spiritual reality and earth. Our state of personal growth is often reflected in these experiences.

Alteration of our senses comes naturally as we develop our sensitivity. Silence initiates the process.

Following are some of the traditional means used to produce temporary changes in consciousness and/or its content. These techniques produce transitory manifestations that are part of our longer-term development:

- Specialized conscious breathing
- Sensory deprivation
- Meditation
- Yoga
- Drumming
- Dancing
- Chanting
- Ecstatic dance
- Hypnosis
- Sonics
- Voice harmonics
- Plants and chemicals

Both positive and negative forces are present in nature and in every realm of existence—physical, psychic, mental, emotional, and spiritual. We enter the astral or psychic world when we transcend the physical plane, entering a slightly more ethereal form of matter containing influences and entities ranging from lowest to highest.

Impressions of all thoughts, feelings, and actions of humankind since the dawn of time are located on the psychic or astral plane.

We draw impressions from the psychic and astral plane by affinity and similarity of vibration. All our thoughts and feelings come to us through the medium of vibrational resonance. What criteria can one use in evaluating and choosing among available techniques to alter our consciousness?

Select ways to access altered states that feel natural and safe for you. Do not explore out of your depth or without proper guidance and support.

Discernment, wisdom, and selectivity about our interactions are crucial when we expand our awareness to include the invisible. We can take control of what we call forward and engage with by requesting that only the beings of the highest vibration and light make themselves known. We can also shield ourselves from any unwanted energies.

Guidance and support are highly recommended when plants or chemicals are used to access astral realms.

Someone who is experienced and capable of stabilizing and directing diverse spiritual energies and traveling to and from astral realms would make a perfect guide.

When we return to ordinary reality, it can be challenging to remember all that has happened in an altered state. Keeping records of these experiences as they occur is important, as much is lost in trying to recall them later.

MAYA WAY

Great Jaguar Paw
Curl Snout
Smoking Frog
Jaguar Paw Skull
Smoking Squirrel
18 Rabbit
Bird Jaguar
Smoke Monkey
Lady Evening star
Lady Great Skull Zero
Flint Sky God
6 Ton Bird Jaguar
Stormy Sky
Lord Water

Rulers of the great Mayan empire at one time or another over the 1600 or so years
Of stories recorded in glyphs and scribed on Steale
Sacred stones strewn throughout the Yucatan and Central America

Smoking Frog, smoking squirrel and smoke monkey may have been early potheads
Potheads with a purpose
I would guess so, since indigenous cultures are rich in the use of herbs for healing and revealing
To this day shamans, healers, diviners, teachers and medicine people
Engage the medicine of the earth to speak to them, heal, show
the way, enlighten, inspire and guide their choices

The Huitchol Indians of northern Mexico are concerned that tourists who travel there to
Harvest and ingest their sacred peyote from its natural growing places
For the experience of a trip
will strip

the area clean of the substance their people have relied upon for hundreds of years as a teacher
and wayshower
Huitchols as you may know create eye dazzling psychedelic arts and crafts
Each person may make one journey in a lifetime to the place of peyote for the visions that will
sustain them as artists – teach them what is true and how to live their lives
The Huitchol elders say that the continuance of their culture relies upon these visions

Smoking Frog, Smoking Squirrel and Smoke Monkey – shamans ancient and modern
Observing how Modern society largely misses out on the expansive nature
of agents of change when they are used Recreationally and without focus, direction or intention
lament the loss – hearing the tingle of the
Keys to our infinite divine nature squandered like an easy,
undeserved and unappreciated inheritance.

Luminous Antonio, 2008

TALKING WITH SPIRITS

All living things have wisdom, a spirit and something worthwhile to communicate. A transfer of energy takes place when we communicate with the spirit world. Shamanic practitioners make a link from the spirit world into this world by becoming a conduit for guiding spirits. The energy or transmission of a spirit can affect the individual practitioner, another person, a group, or the whole world.

Integrated Archaeology involves establishing relationships with invisible worlds and the spirits who inhabit Sacred Places. Establishing a relationship with the spirit world will proceed as any other new relationship might. Who are you speaking with and what do they have to offer? Trust must be in place to be able to work with spirits—use your instinct. This is an interview process and you may have to speak to more than one spirit to find your ideal ally or allies for your explorations.

- Initiate SEEN.
- Use your notebook to record the interaction.
- Write each question and the answer that follows.
- Name the information or quest you have in mind.
- Ask if there is someone available who can answer your questions. Wait for a confirmation—Yes or No.
- Ask if this is an evolved spirit (does not have an ego and isn't involved with opinions, personal agendas and agendas of the world). Have the spirit tell you a little about who they are. An evolved spirit will not seek to control you or interfere with your free will.
- Ask the spirit whether they are a guide or ancestor or other (angel, ascended master, past life friend, faerie, saint, etc.).
- In all cases including contact with an ancestor or relative, it is important that they have gone to the light—reconnected with a higher knowing. Ask if this is so. If not, decline the engagement, thank them, and ask for someone else to step forward.
- Ask if the spirit has a personal agenda.
- Ask whether the spirit has your best interest at heart.
- Does the spirit know what they are talking about and are they capable of responding to the questions you might have?
- Ask if they will identify themselves by name.
- Notice how you feel—is this spirit a loving presence with your best interest at heart? Just as you would in any relationship, use your discernment.

HOW DOES SPIRIT COMMUNICATION FEEL?

Spirits vibrate at a different frequency than humans and energetic changes occur within us when we work with them. Being sensitive to how the communication feels in your body will let you know if there is a potential for overwhelm. Often, the most powerful experiences with the spirit world are very subtle, releasing healing, clarity, and information over time rather than right in the moment.

It is important to feel grounded in any communication with the spirit realm—use SEEN to stabilize and flow any excess energy through your grounding cord into the earth. Our physical being may alter to communicate with spirits. An example might be looking upward with the eyes closed, off to the right with the eyes open.

You may also feel slightly dizzy, lightheaded, very present, and grounded, or highly charged. Notice any physical changes and relax into them—we all have different ways of opening and sustaining communication with the spirit world.

WHAT CAN A SPIRIT TELL ME?

Spirits can act as healers, advisors and teachers, sharing energy and information that has value in many areas of our lives. A spirit teacher often has valuable insights into our unconscious motives, the core of issues and relationships, what steps might be next, or the source of a physical or emotional condition.

Always ask for clarification and more detail. Be receptive to what is given, even if it is not what you want to hear. It may be necessary to take a risk and flow with new information. Speaking with spirits is a relationship that we develop over time.

Trust will also develop as we see the results of information given. Be clear when asking questions of a spirit teacher. In the spirit world all life experiences are considered beneficial as they all have great teachings to impart. You may not be after another learning experience. The question: Should I be in a relationship with this person might more clearly be asked as: Will being in a relationship with this person fulfill my deepest desires for happiness and joy?

HOW DO SPIRITS COMMUNICATE?

Spirits are all unique and may set up a means of communication we do not expect. Smells, words popping into your head, visions, feelings in your body and sounds are some of the ways of spirit communication. The following practice, Writing with Spirit, is an excellent way to initiate contact and carry on a dialogue.

WRITING WITH SPIRIT

The spirit world is available to speak with us and we can initiate communication. Writing with Spirit can be used to access information about a Sacred Place we visit, our relationship to it, or any other questions we may have.

This writing will feel natural and have a flow to it that does not involve the thinking process. Words come quickly into the mind and you need only transcribe them. Once a response to a question is complete, formulate another question. Begin this easy and powerful practice at home and use it anywhere and anytime:

- Reference the Talking to Spirits section of this book and use the process outlined there for establishing the relationship before continuing.
- Choose a quiet place where you are comfortable and will not be disturbed.
- Have a notebook, journal or recording device available.
- Initiate SEEN.
- Close your eyes and formulate a question.
- Write the question in your notebook.
- Write a response to your question—word by word as it is given.
- Allow the words to flow without editing or judging.
- Eliminate any ideas that you are making things up.
- Continue to ask questions, receive answers and to write.
- This is not a time to review what you have written; it is simply a time to ask questions, receive and record the responses. You may feel exhilarated at the speed and clarity of the responses you receive.
- Following are sample questions to begin a dialogue at a Sacred Place:
- Is someone here with me and willing to respond to my questions?
- Have I been at this site in the past?
- What is the true nature and purpose of my journey to this place?
- What have I come here to learn, see, understand, or know?
- What are the lessons I can take with me from the distant past that will cast a positive reflection in my life at this time?
- Where is the strongest energy available to me at this site currently?
- Is there anything I should consider leaving behind or ending as I move forward with my life? Is the letting go mental, emotional, physical or psychic?
- What are some of the components of my new life and reality?
- What am I not seeing?
- Is there healing energy available to me at this site?
- Where is it located?
- How should I access that energy?
- Are there any messages specifically for me from this site?

Be as creative and specific as possible with your questions. The questions you formulate may include some of these and others more specific to your personal quest.

INTERSPECIES COMMUNICATION

Plants, animals, rocks, waters, mountains—indeed, all-natural forms on our planet are alive. We can connect with these beings and exchange information. If you have a pet, using telepathy to send mental pictures to them is a good way to practice. An artifact from a site can be asked about its origin, maker, purpose or age. An example of how to address other species follows:

- Refer to the Entering Sacred Places section of this book to begin.
- Initiate SEEN.
- Create a dialogue as follows using these or similar words:

I ask you to share your wisdom with me, and I invite you to take from me any information that is of value to you. I am grateful to have this opportunity to connect with you and exchange information. I extend my love, gratitude, and blessings to you.

Sacred (mountain, stone, tree, water, being, etc.) who, like myself, holds the memory of all times—I honor you as a magnificent and life-giving being with vast intelligence and wisdom. Although we are in different forms currently, I know we are one, sharing the experience of being on earth.

VOICE HARMONICS

Modern science is now in agreement with what the ancient mystics have told us that everything is in a state of vibration, from the electrons moving around the nucleus of an atom, to planets and distant galaxies moving around stars. As they're creating movement, they are creating vibration, and this vibration can be perceived as sound.

So, everything is creating a sound, including the sofa that we're sitting on, or this table, or our bodies. Every organ, every bone, every tissue, every system of the body is creating a sound. Jonathan Goldman

Our natural voice is a powerful tool for altering our consciousness, clearing the mind, healing the body, connecting with invisible worlds and amplifying awareness. Practice anytime, at home, in the car, lying down, before or after sleeping. The following exercise initiates sonic frequency in the body. Sound is the ancient and future language beyond present-day language forms. Sound emanates from infinite domains. Create and enjoy different vibrational frequencies.

- Find a comfortable place where you can sit or lie down undisturbed.
- Initiate SEEN.
- Take a deep breath in and exhale the sound A (ai).
- Play with vibrating and moving A from the abdomen to the heart, throat, inside the head. You can direct the vibration of any part of the body.
- Change the position of the mouth, open wide and close a little at a time to produce different sounds.
- Move the tongue to the roof of the mouth, bottom of the mouth, curve the tongue. All these positions of the tongue produce different frequencies.
- Have fun exploring how to modulate the sound of A and move it throughout the body.
- Place your hand over the belly, chest, arm, forehead, top of your head while concentrating the sound in that area. Feel the vibration.

- And all subsequent sounds in this exercise can be directed to any area of the body in need of healing or revitalization.

- Work with the other vowels: E, I, O, and U (pronounced uu rather than u—like the vowel sound in "who").

SONIC MEDITATION

Set aside a minimum of fifteen minutes a day to meditate sonically. Use the format above and become familiar with the feeling of being in a sonic resonant field of your own creation. Voice harmonics produce a relaxed, altered state perfect for the exploration of Sacred Places.

12

OUTDOOR AND
SITE ETIQUETTE

YELLOWSTONE NATIONAL PARK*

OUTDOOR AND SITE ETIQUETTE

Natural environments are receiving more visitors all the time, and many are unfamiliar with how to be on the land and preserve it. Whether you plan a day hike or a longer journey, preparation has many phases. Understanding the outdoors and our relationship to it will support us and the magnificent natural environment in which we live.

Those of us who travel to Sacred Places and visit the pristine forests and lands around the world are the natural stewards of these places. No rule, regulation or law has any ability or power to protect and care for these Sacred Places; that is entirely up to those who visit and enjoy them. Our personal role in preserving these sites is crucial to their continued existence. Worldwide, Sacred Places and monuments are increasingly confined due to the heavy traffic of visitors and destructive and disrespectful actions by a few.

BE RESPECTFUL

Sacred Places are the destinations of millions of travelers every year and many sites suffer damage and are negatively affected from the steady stream of visitors.

Climbing on monuments, pyramids, temples, and natural sites accelerates erosion and often causes permanent, irreparable destruction. In many cases, the spirits, ancestors, and guardians will be disturbed. Although climbing is often the practice at a site, and you may see others doing it, avoid climbing, whether they are hills, pyramids, or other structures. Confine your explorations to designated pathways. Reaching the top of an ancient pyramid is not an accomplishment we need to have, especially if our only purpose is to take a picture and say we have been there.

Allow the site to change you; do not attempt to change the site. Do not move things around or take things from the area. Do not leave anything at the site, particularly anything that is not biodegradable. Unless it is clearly the custom, do not leave objects at the site, including visible offerings.

Below are basic guidelines for using the outdoors. Leave No Trace Center for Outdoor Ethics (www.lnt.org) is an excellent resource. Below is material from their site, other wilderness sites and personal experience. Read and become familiar with these guidelines.

PREPARATION – BEFORE YOU GO

- Research and know any regulations and special concerns for the area you will visit.
- Learn about local weather and trail conditions before travel.
- Prepare for extreme weather, hazards, and emergencies.
- Bring appropriate clothing and gear for the climate and areas you will visit.
- Schedule your trip to avoid times of high use.
- Visit in small groups when possible. Consider splitting larger groups into smaller ones. This reduces the impact on the earth.
- Before making a journey, visit your physician to address any concerns about your physical condition.
- Choose destinations you are physically capable of navigating.
- Learn any skills necessary to support your travel experience before you leave home.
- Learn to use any gear or equipment before making the journey.

NAVIGATING TRAILS

- Stay on the trail—protect the native vegetation and reduce erosion by staying on the trail, even if it is muddy.
- Avoid making parallel trails, cutting switchbacks, or widening trails. Low-growing and tiny plants and mosses are delicate and necessary to the environment. Restoration is costly and often fails—it is better to protect the land up front.
- Let others discover wilderness on their own—never mark a new route with blazes or cairns or litter the backcountry with flagging tape.
- Walk in a single file in the middle of the trail, even when wet or muddy.
- Be courteous. Yield to other users on the trail. Step to the downhill side of the trail when meeting pack animals or hikers coming down a hill.
- Use a GPS, map, or compass to eliminate the use of marking paint, rock cairns or flagging.

CAMPING

- Designated camping areas are usually marked by signposts. Camp only in designated camps, along trails, or in the location specified on your permit or otherwise indicated.
- Durable surfaces include established trails and campsites, rock, gravel, dry grasses, or snow. Camp only on durable surfaces.
- Pitch your tent on established bare sites, not on the vegetation.
- Camp at least 200 feet away from lakes and streams to protect riparian areas.
- Altering a site is not necessary. Good campsites are found, not made. Concentrate use on existing campsites.
- Focus activity in areas where vegetation is absent. Keep campsites small. Disperse use to prevent the creation of new campsites and new trails.
- Avoid camping at any places where use is just beginning.
- A collapsible water carrier reduces the number of trips and trampling to a water source and allows you to wash far away from lakes and streams.
- Use small amounts of biodegradable soap for washing yourself or dishes. Carry water at least 200 feet away from streams or lakes and scatter strained dishwater

CAMPFIRE AWARENESS

- Campfires can have a lasting effect on the back country. Use a light-weight stove for cooking. Take along a candle lantern for lighting.
- Fires are not always permitted, check with your local forest service to determine the current situation. When making a fire use established fire rings, a fire plan, or mound fires.
- Control the size of your fire. Keep fires small. Bring your own fire- wood when possible or use sticks from the ground that can be bro- ken by hand.
- Only use dead branches and sticks that have already fallen to the ground.
- Burn your fire down to ash. Put out campfires completely, then scatter cool ashes.
- Douse campfires with water until saturated and no smoke or coals are detectable.
- Cover the fire with dirt or rocks if water to douse it is not available.

DISPOSING OF WASTE

- Whatever you bring in, be sure to pack it back out. Inspect your campsite or other areas of habitation before leaving the area. Remove any spilled foods, trash, litter, or leftover foods—take them with you when you leave.
- Carry a plastic bag on hikes and nature visits and pick up any trash left by others. The psychological message of trash left on the ground is that it is OK to leave more trash. By removing trash, we have an opportunity to help discourage this behavior.
- Dig cat-holes dug 6 to 8 inches deep and located at least 200 feet from any water source, camp, or trails. This is for the deposit of human waste. Cover and disguise the cat-hole when finished.
- Any toilet paper and personal hygiene products should leave the area with you.

LEAVE WHAT YOU FIND

- Examine, look, but do not touch, cultural or historic structures and artifacts. Leaving things, the way you find them will preserve the experience for generations to come.
- Rocks, plants, and other natural objects can be appreciated and explored but leave them as you find them.
- Leave flowers for others to enjoy.
- Take nothing away and leave nothing behind.
- Non-native plants, no matter how beautiful, should be left where they are. Do not transport these species to other locations.
- Do not build structures or furniture in the outdoors.
- Do not dig trenches or alter the landscape in any way.

RESPECT FOR WILDLIFE

- Take in the beauty and grace of wildlife by observing from a distance. Allow them the freedom to be as they are. Do not follow, approach, or capture them.
- Never feed wild animals. Feeding wildlife puts them at risk in many ways. Their health is compromised, natural behaviors are altered, and exposure to predators and other dangers ensues.
- Store all food and trash securely to protect wildlife.
- Always control pets or leave them at home. It is not safe to allow pets to run unleashed or uncontrolled—there are wild animals out there and small animals are vulnerable to attack.
- Mating, nesting, raising young and certain seasons are extremely sensitive times for wildlife. Stay away from their habitations and nests.

CONSIDER OTHER VISITORS

- Show respect for other visitors in the outdoors and protect the quality of their experience.
- Camp away from other visitors, respecting their private space and creating private space for yourself.
- Enjoy the symphony of nature's sounds—let them prevail. Lower your voice and avoid loud voices and loud noises.
- Electronic equipment can be limited to what is necessary, like the ability to call for help if there is an emergency. Wilderness is a respite from modern technological society— enjoy the solitude of the outdoors.
- Be safe
- If you plan to hike or visit a remote area, be sure to let someone know where you are going and how long you plan to be gone.
- Take adequate water and whatever other supplies you might need in case of being lost or an emergency.
- Be sure to have layers of clothing for warmth, if needed.
- Determine whether the area you will be hiking or visiting has cell phone service.
- When traveling with a guide or tour company to remote areas, determine whether communication devices are in place to call for help if there is an emergency.
- Pack a small medical kit.

13

A BRIEF
HISTORY OF
ARCHAEOLOGY

GOBEKLI TEPI, TURKEY*

ARCHAEOLOGICAL DIG*

A BRIEF HISTORY OF ARCHAEOLOGY

A human somewhere in the vast expanse of time that came before a word was written down or carved into stone, suddenly got the idea to dig around. As he or she explored, they attempted to reveal or procure a remnant of the past.

Maybe they were just the curious type, driven by boredom and with time on their hands. Or perhaps they had an inkling that something valuable was there to be uncovered? At any rate they likely picked up a stick or rock and began to dig. The identity of this person will never be known, but we can rest assured that they existed and that after them many others would come.

We can imagine these early explorers wandering into caves, finding walls filled with astonishing artwork. What questions arose in their minds? Who were these people? Where are they now? Such discoveries whether random and accidental or purposeful, highlights a very human need to know where we came from, or perhaps more correctly, who came before us?

The history of archaeology as a study of the ancient past had its beginnings at least as early as the Mediterranean Bronze Age (3900 BC), where we find the first archaeological investigations of ruins.

Alongside this curiosity for history would come a less noble behavior - looting. We know for example that the tombs of pharaohs were plundered by ancient grave robbers hoping for financial gain in exchange for their finds. Enquiry and plunder as twin forces impacted excavations from the get-go.

The reason is simple. There has always been a market for ancient artifacts, and this helped to fund many religious crusades and land conquests through-out the ages. Wholesale looting of the ancient artifacts of other peoples were legitimized and sanctioned by elite rulers, secular and religious. This type of activity was pretty consistent right up until the second study of Pompeii and Herculaneum in the early 1700's.

Then, during the 15th and 16th centuries, an appreciation of ancient art and the desire to collect antiquities for their intrinsic value, inspired the systematic mining of ancient Roman and Greek sites. However, the idea that these uncovered items were historically significant to humanity in general had not yet universally emerged.

Remarkably, and perhaps ironically, archaeology as a scientific study is only about 150 years old. Back then, it was mostly the wealthy, educated Westerner that organized archaeological digs in faraway lands. Consequently, their cultural biases and opinions often dictated agendas.

For example, enormous amounts of ancient artifacts were dug up and removed from their sacred resting sites and transported to museums in Europe. The opinions and biases of these early archaeologists would form and shape our ideas about humanity's past down to today.

Yet, we should not so readily dismiss the significance of what many of our early modern archaeologists uncovered. Their curiosity and foibles revealed the sites, put them on the map and opened insight into our past.

ARCHAEOLOGICAL ADVANCEMENTS AND TECHNIQUES

It is important to thread the needle and show how humans in more recent times have attempted to understand our distant past. This list serves as a brief overview of techniques that became standard practice in modern archaeology.

- First recorded guide to the ruins of ancient Rome: Flavio Biondo, early 15th century
- Utilized folklore and methodically documented a world heritage site: Stonehenge and environs, John Aubrey 1640s
- First recorded supervised excavation: Marcello Venuti 1730s
- Employed wedge sampling to examine the stratigraphy: Thomas Jefferson 1780s
- Discovered Rosetta Stone, deciphered hieroglyphics: Napoleon Bonaparte, Francois Champollion 1801
- Coined archaeological terminology: Richard Colt-Hoare 1812s
- Uncovered ancient Egypt: Giovanni Battista Belzoni 1812s
- Used classical texts to locate excavation sites: Heinrich Schliemann 1860s
- Developed seriation: William Flinders Petrie 1880s
- Transported Minoan artifacts to be studied by Classicists: Sir Arthur Evans 1900s
- Discovered the most widely recognized archaeological site in recent history, the intact tomb of the 18th Dynasty Pharaoh, Tutankhamun: Howard Carter 1920s.

PROMINENT ARCHAEOLOGISTS

FLAVIO BIONDO

(1392–1463) was an Italian Renaissance man: historian, humanist who:

- Divided history into three parts: Ancient, Medieval, Modern.
- Had the ability to see important historical sites where others saw ruins.
- Used topography to map changes through time in one area.
- Understood the value of preserving and cataloguing these areas.

JOHN AUBREY

(1626–1697), a British gentleman who:

- Investigated Stonehenge and other stone circles in the 17th century CE and understood their significance.
- Methodically and systematically arranged for megalithic sites to be mapped and preserved.
- Studied folklore to connect his finds with a cultural past.
- Left an invaluable record of preserved histories.

MARCEL VENUTI

an antiquarian, during 1738 who:

- Reopened the shafts at Herculaneum.
- Supervised excavations and translated inscriptions.
- Proved the site was in fact, Herculaneum
- Authored in 1750, *A Description of the First Discoveries of the Ancient City of Heraclea.*

WILLIAM FLINDERS PETRIE

(1853–1942) British gentleman, modern archaeologist who:

- While working in Egypt developed the concept of seriation, permitting accurate dating long before scientific methods were available to corroborate his chronologies.
- As a meticulous excavator and a scrupulous record keeper, established many of the habits and ideas behind modern archaeological recording.

MARGARET MURRAY

Breaking glass ceilings

Margaret Murray (1863–1963) was a British archaeologist and scholar, who emerged in the late 19th century as a formidable figure in the developing specialty of Egyptology. In 1899 she became the first female lecturer in archaeology in the UK, teaching at the University College London. She led excavations in Malta, Menorca and Palestine, according to a study published in the journal Archaeology International, 2013.

GERTRUDE CATON THOMPSON
Revolutionized excavation practice
Gertrude Caton Thompson (1888–1985) began her archaeological pursuits at age thirty-three, leading Neolithic and Paleolithic excavations in Egypt, Yemen, and Zimbabwe. Her 1929 Zimbabwe dig was excavated entirely by women. Her methods, which included meticulous soil scrutiny and noting objects' positions relative to each other, revolutionized the way that sites were surveyed and studied.

DOROTHY GARROD
First used aerial photography
Paleolithic archaeologist Dorothy Garrod (1892–1968), uncovered important findings about early human origins, including the first evidence of the Middle Stone Age, and the first evidence of dog domestication. She was also the first person to use aerial photographs for archaeological work.

HONOR FROST
Aquatic archaeology
Honor Frost (1917–2010) was the first to usher in an era of underwater archaeology. Frost incorporated archaeology with her love of deep-sea diving, leading dives and organizing excavations of sites and shipwrecks in the Mediterranean. Her dives included the discovery of the lost palace of Alexander and Ptolemy in the Port of Alexandria.

GUDRUN CORVINUS
Vertebrate paleontology, Paleolithic archaeology
Gudrun Corvinus (1932–2006), a Paleontologist, geologist, and archaeologist researched and excavated sites across Asia and Africa. Her discoveries informed the understanding of vertebrate paleontology and Paleolithic archaeology.

In the 1970s, Corvinus was part of the team in Ethiopia that discovered "Lucy," the partial skeleton of a human ancestor known as Australopithecus afarensis, a hominin that lived 3.2 million years ago. She later discovered Paleolithic sites in Ethiopia that were determined to be "among the oldest archaeological evidence in the world," and unearthed numerous Paleolithic sites in India, Nepal and Tibet.

THERESA SINGLETON
African Diaspora
Writer and archaeologist, Theresa Singleton (b. 1952) was a pioneer of historical archaeology in North America. Her work uncovered important findings representing the

African Diaspora, particularly African American history and culture under slavery, and life in communities of African Americans descended from former slaves.

WHITNEY BATTLE-BAPTISTE
Reconstructing archaeology
Whitney Battle-Baptiste, an American historical archaeologist of African and Cherokee descent, is an important pioneer in reconstructing and interpreting life for African Americans through exploration of African American family homesteads and domestic spaces of enslaved Africans. In her book "Black Feminist Archaeology" (Left Coast Press, 2011), Battle-Baptiste proposed improving modern practices of historical archaeology through principles of Black feminism and challenges the field of archaeology to develop greater sensitivity toward questions of gender and race.

DAME KATHLEEN MARY KENYON
One of the most influential archaeologists of the 20th century
Dame Kathleen Mary Kenyon, (1906–1978) was a leading British archaeologist of Neolithic culture in the Fertile Crescent. She is best known for her excavations of Tell es-Sultan, the site of ancient Jericho, from 1952 to 1958, and has been called one of the most influential archaeologists of the 20th century.

ZELIA MARIA MAGDALENA NUTTALL
Pioneer in pre-Aztec artefacts
Zelia Maria Magdalena Nuttall (1857, San Francisco–1933, Coyoacán, Mexico) was an American archaeologist and anthropologist specialized in pre-Aztec Mexican cultures and pre-Columbian manuscripts. She discovered two forgotten manuscripts of this type in private collections, one of them being the Codex Zouche-Nuttall. She was one of the first to identify and recognize artefacts dating back to the pre-Aztec period.

LINDA SCHELE
Deciphering Mayan hieroglyphs
Linda Schele (1942–1998) was an expert in the field of Maya epigraphy and iconography. She played an invaluable role in the decipherment of many Maya hieroglyphs. She produced a massive volume of drawings of stelae and inscriptions, which, following her wishes, are free for use to scholars today.

Women archaeologists have too often been overlooked, under-represented, or written out of history entirely. Their ground-breaking contributions are now rightly being acknowledged.

SOURCES AND FURTHER READING
Trowelblazers.com
Brown.edu/Research/Breaking Ground

KILKA CULTURE, BENEATH CUZCO, PERU

DIFFERENT TYPES OF ARCHAEOLOGY

There are also different branches of archaeology.

Traditional Archaeology is also known as Cultural-Historical archaeology. Knowledge of ancient, prehistoric and extinct cultures is derived from a scientific study of material remains of past human life and activities. Human artifacts such as pottery, tools, bones, jewelry, stone walls, implements, fabrics and monuments to name a few, are collected from earliest shelters, tombs, temples, pyramids; any previous habitat. Objects are removed from the place which they lay and data is analyzed apart from the context from which the artifacts are drawn. Artifacts are catalogued, analyzed and placed in a chronology of archaeological record.

Processual Archaeology evolved during the 1960s. In this discipline all the data is still important to the processual archaeologist, but the facts are only a piece of the puzzle. A further step here is to develop an explanation of how the people who created or owned such artifacts lived and thought.

Post-Processual Archaeology challenges cultural-historical and processual archaeology stating that we cannot know the lifestyle and belief systems of ancient cultures while interpreting through a modern lens

Alternative Archeology, New Thought and Revisionist Archaeology are considered by the traditional community to be pseudo-archaeology; offering interpretations of the past from outside of the archaeological community and has no method-based proof for its claims (as yet).

Note: it's good to put this into context here. Because conventional scientists can find no connection between the positions of stars and human behavior, astronomy is classified as pseudoscience. Naturopathic medicine was also portrayed as a pseudoscience after scientific trials proved many of the theory's claims to be wrong. Feng-shui is highly regarded in China but considered pseudoscience because of its superstitious elements. Flood geology is a part of pseudoscience since scientific efforts have yet to prove the occurrence of a global flood. In other words, sometimes science needs to play catch-up.

Here is a list of some researchers and pioneers in the Alternative Archaeology sector:

- **Dr J.J. Hurtak**, Ph.D., Ph.D., M.A., M.Th. Social scientist, futurist, remote sensing and space law specialist and author of twenty books, his best-seller is The Keys of Enoch®.

- **Desiree Hurtak**, Ph.D., MS.Sc. Social scientist, futurist, and co-founder with her husband Dr. J.J. Hurtak of The Academy for Future Science, an international organization working in over fifteen countries. Dr. Desiree Hurtak is also an environmentalist and an author of several books.

- **Zacharia Sitchen**, author and biblical scholar and one of the few scholars able to read and interpret ancient Sumerian and Akkadian clay tablets. His controversial theories of the Anunnaki origins of humanity have been translated into 20 languages.

- **Graham Hancock**, recognized as an unconventional thinker who raises controversial questions about humanity's past. His books have sold more than five million copies worldwide and have been translated into 27 languages.

- **Michael Cremo,** co-author with Dr. Richard L. Thompson of *Forbidden Archaeology: The Hidden History of the Human Race* "shows that archaeologists and anthropologists over the past 150 years have accumulated vast amounts of evidence showing that humans like ourselves have existed on this planet for tens of millions of years. They show how evidence has been suppressed, ignored and forgotten because it contradicts generally-held ideas about human evolution."

- **Dr. Robert Schoch**, Ph.D., M.Phil., M.S. In the early 1990s, Dr. Schoch stunned the world with his revolutionary research that recast the date of the Great Sphinx of Egypt to a period thousands of years earlier than its standard attribution.

- **Andrew Collins**, a science and history writer, and the author of over a dozen books that challenge the way we perceive the past.

- **Chris Dunn**, author of *Lost Technologies of Ancient Egypt: Advanced Engineering in the Temples of the Pharaohs* which describes a holistic energy device that is harmonically coupled with the Earth and its inhabitants. Another book, *The Giza Power Plant: Technologies of Ancient Egypt.*

- **Dr. Carmen Boulter** is Director, Producer, and Writer of *The Pyramid Code*, an epic five-episode documentary series that has aired on national TV.

- **John Antony West**, foremost exponent of the 'Symbolist' school of Egyptology which sees (and demonstrates) an ancient sacred science where modern academics see mainly superstition. He re-dated the Great Sphinx of Giza via geology, (proving that it must be at least 10,000 years old or older). Author of non-fiction books on Egypt.

- **Marie D. Jones**, best-selling author of over 20 non-fiction books on disaster preparedness, the paranormal, ancient knowledge, unknown mysteries, UFOs and alien technology, surveillance and technology, conspiracy theories, metaphysics, spirituality and cutting-edge science.

- **Laird Scranton**, an independent software designer who became interested in Dogon mythology and symbolism in the early 1990s. He has studied ancient myth, language, and cosmology since 1997 and authored several books on the subject.

- **Oana R. Ghiocel**, an independent producer, filmmaker and consultant who produced on her own three feature length documentary films plus short docs, screened around the world.

- **Kathryn Denning** Ph.D., is an Associate Professor of Anthropology at York University, where she teaches courses ranging from the Anthropology of Outer Space to Archaeology and Society and the Anthropology of Im/mortality. Her Ph.D. was in Archaeology and Prehistory, but since 2004 her research has focused on the social issues connected to astrobiology and SETI, Mars simulations, the evolution of intelligence and civilizations on Earth, and contemporary ideas concerning the colonization of space.

- **Gary A. David**, researcher and author of *The Orion Zone: Ancient Star Cities of the American Southwest* and other books on the theory of ancient civilizations.

- **Paul Devereux**, founding co-editor of *Time and Mind - Journal of Archaeology, Consciousness and Culture*. His mix of archaeological, anthropological and consciousness studies have inspired several books.

- **David Hatcher Childress**. His forte in writing focuses mainly on suppressed technology, secret technologies, lost cities, time travel and cryptozoology and he has authored 20 books on this subject.

- **Robert G. Bauval**. Involved in alternative history, researcher and writer of *The Orion Mystery* and many other books on the mysteries and knowledge of the past.

ABOUT THE AUTHOR

Luminous Antonio is a lifelong world traveler and researcher of ancient archaeological sites and Sacred Places. For the past three decades, Luminous has guided groups on journeys to Sacred Places around the world.

She coined the term"Integrative Archaeology". In her words:

"I believe we are descended from god(s) and we are gods who have forgotten our true essence and capabilities. I hold the certainty that we, as a species, and the remains of our pasts—sacred sites and power places—are much older and more advanced than we have been led to believe. As we connect with our ancestral homes and earthly locations, we can reignite pivotal memories, raise consciousness, awareness, heal ourselves and re-establish our original divinity. Integrative Archaeology gives us tools to explore within and at Sacred Places to actualize an exquisite existence".

BACKGROUND

Her interest in the past was first reflected in the years she spent brokering 18th- 20th Century European and American Paintings, period furniture, handmade carpets, fine art and jewelry to private clients and through auction rooms in New York, including Sotheby's, Christies and Doyle's. After moving West in 1980, she furthered her art education earning two degrees (Painting and Performance/Video) at the San Francisco Art Institute. Her visual and multi-media art speaks of inner worlds and unseen dimensions.

Her fine art can be seen at:
LuminousAntonioFineArt.com.

As an innovator in the use of Tibetan and Crystal Bowls and Voice Harmonics, Luminous founded X-Static Sound Research and Development in 1984, focused on consciousness expansion and the healing properties of sonics.

The Integrative Archaeology Foundation 501(c)(3) dedicated to supporting indigenous cultures to maintain their language, rituals, ceremonies, traditions and lands, was established by Luminous in 2012.

Luminous Antonio is a member of the Institute of Mayan Studies (InstituteofMayanStudies.org), Archaeological Institute of America (Archaeological.org), Arizona Archaeological Society (azarchsoc.org), Society of American Archaeology (saa.org), and the Archaeological Conservatory (ArchaeologicalConservatory.org).

Through her new platform, LuminousAntonioAuthor.com, Luminous will present this book and others as they become available.

Sacred Places allow spiritual communication—are human freeways to remembrance of our Eternal Divine Self.

Luminous Antonio

PORTALS of TRANSCENDENCE
P U B L I S H I N G

www.LuminousAntonio.com

www.ingramcontent.com/pod-product-compliance
Lightning Source LLC
Chambersburg PA
CBHW060519130626
46553CB00002B/564